Effective Writing Skills for Social Work Students

Effective Writing Skills for Social Work Students

PHIL MUSSON

Series Editors: Jonathan Parker and Greta Bradley

LearningMatters

Published in 2011 by Learning Matters Ltd.

British Library Cataloguing in Publication Data
A CIP record for this book is available from the British Library.

ISBN: 978 0 85725 417 7

This book is also available in the following formats:
Adobe ebook ISBN: 978 0 85725 419 1
EPUB ebook ISBN: 978 0 85725 418 4
Kindle ISBN: 978 0 85725 420 7

Cover and text design by Code 5 Design Associates Ltd
Project management by Deer Park Productions
Typeset by Pantek Arts Ltd, Maidstone, Kent
Printed and bound in Great Britain by MPG Books Group, Bodmin, Cornwall

Learning Matters Ltd
20 Cathedral Yard
Exeter EX1 1HB
Tel: 01392 215560
info@learningmatters.co.uk
www.learningmatters.co.uk

Contents

vi

Series Editors' Preface

The Western world, including the UK, face numerous challenges over forthcoming years. These include dealing with the impact of an increasingly ageing population, with its attendant social care needs and working with the financial implications that such a changing demography brings. At the other end of the life-span the need for high quality child care, welfare and safeguarding services have been highlighted as society develops and responds to a changing complexion.

Migration has developed as a global phenomenon and we now live and work with the implications of international issues in our everyday and local lives. Recession and retention, and the impact of conflicts, both distant and proximal, also impact on the social and health care needs of populations. Often these issues influence how we construct our social services and determine what services we need to offer. It is likely that as a social worker you will work with a diverse range of people throughout your career, many of whom have experienced significant, even traumatic, events that require a professional and caring response. As well as working with individuals, however, you may be required to respond to the needs of a particular community disadvantaged by world events or excluded within local communities because of assumptions made about them.

The importance of social work education came to the fore again following the inquiry into the death of baby Peter and the subsequent report from the Social Work Task Force set up in its aftermath. It is timely, also, to reconsider elements of social work education as is being taken forward by the Reform Board process in England – indeed, we should view this as a continual striving for excellence! Reflection, revision and reform allow us to focus clearly on what knowledge is useful to engage with in learning to be a social worker. A core aspect of both education and practice relates to the ability to write effectively in, about and for practice; a skill that is honed and further developed in qualifying education. This book lends weight to the importance of writing as a central professional activity.

The books in this series repond to the agendas driven by changes brought about by professional body, Government and disciplinary review. They aim to build on and offer introductory texts based on up-to-date knowledge and to help communicate this in an accessible way preparing the ground for future study as you develop your social work career. The books are written by people passionate about social work and social services and aim to instil that passion on others. Within these challenging social and political contexts this book is important for all social workers in all fields of practice as they seek to reaffirm social work's commitment to those it serves and to ensure other social work commands the respect of other professionals with whom practitioners work.

Professor Jonathan Parker, Bournemouth University
Greta Bradley, University of York

Acknowledgements

I would like to thank the editorial team from Learning Matters for their advice, support and guidance, and the numerous educators, colleagues and students who have contributed to my learning and continue to do so.

Introduction

My overarching aim in writing this book is to communicate with you, the reader, and to communicate in a clear, unambiguous manner that writing well matters, that it is important. I want you to consider the quality of your written expression as a form of how you present yourself. Irrespective of whether you are on an undergraduate or a master's programme or undertaking post-qualification studies, I want to encourage you to enjoy writing and to take pride in your written expression. In short, I want to ignite your enthusiasm to express yourself as well as you can at present and to strive to improve. The information contained in the book, if learnt from and employed, will help you develop the skills to write well. Most pieces of writing can be improved upon. Ultimately, 'the end' of a piece of work has to come if it is ever to be finished, so a compromise has to be struck. However, a piece of work may still be as good as it can be even within the constraints of time, effort and skills available.

Although you are likely to be currently engaged in a process of vocational qualification, or post-qualifying study, you will soon come to realise that the social worker is never 'trained' but is engaged in a process of continual professional development that will last the length of a career. Accordingly, you will not make a better investment in that career than learning how to write well at this point. This book is not written solely for students embarking on a qualifying degree in social work but also for practitioners involved in higher education through undertaking post-qualifying courses. Students should find this book highly relevant to their learning where they are required to express themselves in writing, but specifically in writing academically and for competence-based assessments and portfolios of practice.

The first chapter, 'Writing for university', is for students engaged in pre- and post-qualifying courses and addresses the academic component of writing at university. The skills required to write well at university are identified and you will be invited to undertake an appraisal of the skills you have so as to better identify areas for development. The chapter has an emphasis on how to achieve a good standard of written English and uses exercises and case studies to illustrate the correct use of grammar and punctuation. It includes guidance on interpreting the assignment task and understanding what is required. Errors that constitute academic offences are explained and the chapter concludes with advice regarding the presentation of your work.

The second chapter, 'Placement preparation and practice', is dedicated to issues concerning practice placements. It begins with identifying the criteria your practice will be assessed against while on placement and stresses the importance of acquiring a working appreciation of the occupational standards students are required to achieve. Consideration is given to placement choice, location and some practical factors when on placement. Important personnel and their roles within the placement structure are identified, as are significant meetings during the placement and the importance of preparing for them. The chapter concludes with examples of problems on placements and how to avoid them.

The third chapter, 'Writing for practice placements', considers the skills required to write a good portfolio of practice. The chapter builds upon the first chapter, as a good standard of written English is essential in effective written communication but writing a portfolio of practice presents particular challenges that merit specific consideration. The first of these is concerned with claiming evidence of having met the National Occupational Standards and Values Requirements, which is explored, and examples of good practice are given using case studies. The challenge of referring to work undertaken with service users while preserving their identity is discussed and a way of achieving this is proposed. The difference between writing descriptively, analytically and critically and when to use these styles appropriately is considered, as is the need to show how theory and particular knowledge have been applied; case studies are used to provide examples of how best to do this. The chapter concludes with the requirement to demonstrate reflection in practice, and again examples are used to show how best to do this.

All three chapters contain information that can make a valuable and effective contribution to the quality of students' work on pre- and post-qualifying courses in both assignments and portfolios of practice.

There are agreed and specified occupational standards, codes of conduct and statements about the knowledge, skills and values that together describe the professional landscape of social work in England and Wales in the twenty-first century. This book draws on some of these to demonstrate how to navigate this landscape to achieve professional qualification. There are some general themes and examples given about a number of features common to qualifying courses. However, the reader's attention is drawn to the fact that there are likely to be minor differences in preferences for referencing systems, arrangements for undertaking placements and methods for the gathering of evidence according to the particular Higher Education Institution attended. This does not detract from the value of understanding the enduring principles involved in writing well and submitting assignments and portfolios of good quality and to a high standard. Students need to apply these enduring principles through the particular requirements as stipulated by the governing bodies of the day and the institution they are attending.

Chapter 1

Writing for university

A C H I E V I N G   A   D E G R E E   I N   S O C I A L   W O R K

This chapter will help you meet the following National Occupational Standards.
Key Role 6: Demonstrate professional competence in social work practice.
It will also introduce you to the academic standards set out in the following social work subject benchmark statement:
5.6 **Communication skills.**

Introduction

In this Learning Matters series 'Transforming Social Work Practice', it is customary to identify which key roles of the National Occupational Standards and benchmark statements of the Quality Assurance Agency for Higher Education are relevant to the particular chapter under consideration. Accordingly, Key Role 6: *Demonstrate professional competence in social work practice* and Benchmark Statement 5.6: *Write accurately and clearly in styles adapted to the audience, purpose and context of the communication* are cited as having specific relevance to this chapter. However, as writing is such a fundamental means of communication, being sufficiently skilled to communicate effectively in writing is an essential generic skill. At the time of writing, social work practices are again under revision. The Social Work Task Force reported in 2009; its recommendations are poised for various levels of implementation, so the key roles and practice curricula are likely to change. Nevertheless, the ability to write to a good professional standard will remain an essential skill whatever changes come about. It may well be that included in the changes is a greater emphasis on the ability to write well. I was talking to two senior managers of a local authority's children's services recently and they were bemoaning the fact that they would reject a significant number of applications for social work posts from newly qualified social workers, purely on the grounds of the poor standard of written English. Make sure your application is in the 'invite for interview' pile, not in the bin!

The contents of this chapter will help you develop and improve your writing skills. The role your motivation plays in contributing to work of quality is highlighted before the skills required to write well are identified. The opportunity for you to undertake an appraisal of your current skills is presented, which is followed by the requirements for achieving a good standard of written English. The chapter concludes with issues regarding presentation, including addressing the assignment question, plagiarism and preparing your work for submission.

Effort + Time + Application of skills = Work of quality

Unfortunately for those of us who like to cut corners where possible, this equation holds true and there are no substitutes for its factors. Whether you want to work hard to achieve a first class degree or 'do enough to get by' and obtain a third, or something in between, you will need to pass assignments to be awarded your degree. Your time and that of your tutors is precious so you might as well try your best to achieve a good pass at the first attempt. However, this will require effort, time and the successful application of a number of skills. If you are unaccustomed to writing for an academic discipline you are unlikely to possess these skills at the point of enrolment, but the good news is that they can be acquired within a short timescale, so long as you understand what is required. Even if you already have these skills, to a basic level, they can usually be improved upon. If you have these skills to a competent level, they can often be honed. If there is no room for improvement, you probably do not need this book, or any other come to that!

In essence, this book suggests that the acquisition of competent academic writing skills is dependent on two variables: effort and time. Effort, in this context, may be described as a determined attempt and a desire to succeed. Effort has the potential to involve hard work and it probably will, but how hard you find this and the extent to which you feel it to be a struggle can be linked to how you feel about the subject and the quality of your final draft. It will be easier if you like or enjoy the subject and you care about the quality of your product. In this sense, effort is inextricably linked to your motivation.

Time, there is never quite enough of it, is there? Today, students are busy people, often balancing demands on their time through work, family and friends, competing modules and having a life! However, achieving a good mark for an assignment will involve reading around the subject and thinking about it as well as writing the assignment. An approximate idea of the amount of study time a subject might require can be calculated by multiplying the academic credit rating of the module by a factor of 10. For example, a module whose assessment is worth 15 academic credits may be considered as requiring 150 hours of study on the part of the student in order to be in a position to achieve a good pass. This figure includes lecture and seminar time spent on the subject.

So, having identified that the acquisition of academic writing skills, like any skill, is a function of time and effort, let us move on to consider these skills in more detail.

Identifying the skills required in writing for university

You will need the following generic skills to write successfully for university. These have been grouped into three skill sets:

1. *The ability to write in an academic style.*

Students come to university with a range of written communication skills. These may include, for example, texting and writing for pleasure, but may not include a high level of skill in writing in an academic style. This style is characterised by: the focus on specific objectives or learning outcomes; accurate description, a degree of analysis, qualified objectivity and critical appraisal; the absence of colloquial expression; representing and offering informed commentary on the attributed views of others; a good standard of written English. We will consider these characteristics in more detail later on.

2. *The ability to comprehend competing theories of explanation or argument.*

During your course of study you will come across a range of ideas, some of which claim to offer, to varying degrees, explanations of a variety of phenomena around us. Some of these ideas appear to, and indeed do, conflict, compete and complement each other. Students need to be able to think about such ideas and come to a substantiated view of the contribution they make to our understanding.

3. *The ability to find, use and attribute an appropriate and relevant range of source material.*

It is vital that students can use learning and library resources effectively. Universities offer information in a variety of modes, and will explain to students how to research and use the learning resources to which students may have access. They will also produce specific information on the system of referencing source material that students are required to use in their assignments. The Harvard referencing system appears to be becoming universally accepted but this cannot be assumed and different universities may use an alternative system or make minor changes in the way their system is applied. Therefore students need to learn how to apply the referencing system used in their particular university so as to not lose marks for poor referencing.

The individual skills contained in these three 'skill sets' are not usually acquired quickly but are part of the developmental process students undergo as they become competent in learning to learn in higher education, which usually occurs over the course of study. What should the student concentrate on first? All the skills contained in the skill sets are required at some level to pass the first assignment. Skill set 3 is required at a basic level from the time you start researching for your first assignment. This is why universities include sessions on how to use their library and learning resources within their induction programmes during what are often called 'Induction' or 'Freshers' Week'. You are strongly advised to attend such sessions. Help with the acquisition of the skills in sets 1 and 2 are often less structured, hence the need for this book.

The words used to describe the skills in set 1 are formal but should not be shied away from as this is the language used in academic study. Any fear they evoke can be dispelled by understanding what the terms mean and scheduling time for you, the student, to become competent in their usage. The classification of the degree a student is awarded is usually calculated from the marks their assignments merited during the second and third or final year. This reflects and is sympathetic toward the developmental process mentioned earlier by allowing time for the student to become a competent learner during the first year, prior to the marks achieved contributing toward the classification of the final degree.

Your degree will comprise 360 academic credit points. This number will be achieved through progressive accumulation over the number of academic years your programme is scheduled to run for and your progress towards this will be ratified at your institution's exam board held at the end of each academic year. The learning you will be undertaking over the course of your study is likely to be modular in structure. Each of the modules or units you will be studying will be listed in the course structure and timetabled accordingly. The tutors for these modules usually produce a module handbook, which describes the module and its specification, including its academic credit point rating and, equally important, specific objectives or learning outcomes. What do these terms mean: 'specific objectives or learning outcomes'? Usually the module description, presented in the module handbook, or module specification, will contain a set of anticipated learning outcomes. It will say something like: By the end of your study on this module you will be able to do or understand x, y and z. For example: 'By the end of your study on Using Theory and Methods in Social Work you will have been introduced to a number of theories of explanation and had the opportunity to apply a variety of methods of inter-vention to practice scenarios'. What better way for you to demonstrate this than by using the learning outcomes as the criteria, often termed 'specific assessment criteria', against which your assignment is marked? So, this is what often happens: the specific objectives you are expected to have learned about upon completing the module are the same or similar to those you are asked to write about in the assessment for that module, which are also the same or similar to the criteria your work will be marked against. This modular approach is an effective method of breaking down the total amount of learning required for a professional qualification, for an occupation such as social work, into bite-size chunks. The module handbooks or specifications are significant documents in the learning process you are undertaking and you are well advised to read them at the beginning of the period of study to which they refer.

It's all about style: How to make your work look good

Accurate description

This term identifies a skill that most students have acquired by the time they enrol at university. It is the ability to say how something appears to be, or description of what people did or what took place.

A degree of analysis

This term builds on the ability to provide a description by going on to offer an explanation of why something appears to be the way, or ways, it does. This skill is often developed through the first year and early part of the second year.

Qualified objectivity

This term describes an ability to develop and represent informed opinion, rather than simply expressing our own. It is 'qualified' because we can never completely divest ourselves of our personal values but we can be aware of the role they may play in influencing our attempts to be objective in applying theoretical frameworks to what we see around us.

Critical appraisal

This term describes the ability to build on the skills of describing and analysing by going on to offer an evaluation of the extent to which an idea or theory takes our understanding further and explains why things are as they appear, or how they could be in different circumstances. This skill is often developed as the student gains confidence in their ability to learn and engage, in a scholarly way, with what they are learning and this skill often develops during the second year and early part of the third; however, these timescales are generalisations.

Absence of colloquial expression

This phase relates to a requirement for academic writing. You may describe over a drink and a chat with a friend, how you met someone and 'clicked with' them, implying that you felt you had 'made a connection' and had 'got on' with them. This is an example of a colloquial expression, and appropriate for your chat with a friend. When writing academically, you would need to write in terms of 'engaging' or 'establishing a relationship' with the other person in which you 'communicated effectively'.

Representing and offering informed commentary on the attributed views of others

This relates to how you use the work of other writers in your own work. Other people's ideas, theories, writings, etc., belong to them and are their 'intellectual property' so using this work without attributing it to them, 'the owner', is considered a form of theft and an academic offence called *plagiarism*. It must be avoided, and ways of properly using the work of others will be discussed later in this book.

ACTIVITY 1.1

Think about this list of the skills identified as being required to successfully write for university. Using the list, undertake an appraisal of your current skills with the list and identify what skills, if any, you may need to develop. An example is given below.

Skills Appraisal

Skill	Needs developing	Already possess, fairly competent	Already possess, good level of competence
Ability to analyse	Not confident about this – needs developing		

Continued

ACTIVITY *1.1* continued

Ability to accurately describe		Feel fairly confident	
Ability to write to a good standard of English			Quite confident about this

Your Skills Appraisal

Skill	Needs developing	Already possess, fairly competent	Already possess, good level of competence

If you have identified any skill gaps or areas of skill that require developing, design or complete an action plan like the one offered in Activity 1.2.

An example of a skill audit action plan is given below.

Skills Audit Action Plan

Skill to be developed	Target date	How you will achieve it	How you will know you have achieved it
Ability to analyse	End of 2nd term 1st year	Undertake study skills exercise at uni. Practise as an independent learner	Self-assessment. Feedback on assignment. Discussion in tutorials

Your Skills Audit Action Plan

Skill to be developed	Target date	How you will achieve it	How you will know you have achieved it

Continued

The key points in this section have been:

- *The identification of the skills required to write successfully at university. These skills are essential for writing successfully at university.*

- *An appraisal of the skills you have. Self-appraisal is an important skill in itself and you may have been pleasantly surprised at the result. In addition to helping identify areas for development it is also important to recognise the skills you already have.*

- *An action plan to develop the skills you need to acquire. Actions plans can, if unwieldy, have a similar fate to many New Year's resolutions so keep them small, focused and achievable within a realistic time frame.*

- *The acquisition of these skills to a good standard is an investment not solely for your degree but for your career and ultimately yourself.*

Achieving a good standard of written English

A thing of beauty is a joy forever, so said John Keats in his poem of which this is the first line. It is uncertain if a well-written sentence may be regarded a thing of beauty. However, a well-written sentence can give the author a sense of satisfaction, in terms of ability and clarity of expression. It allows the reader to comprehend what was written without having to try to work out the intended meaning. Consider these two sentences:

> *Statement One: Social workers look to engage service users who are viewed as vulnerable or in need due to their struggling to participate in society fully for whatever reason.*

> *Statement Two: Social work is undertaken with those who are marginalised in society, the dispossessed, the dysfunctional and those in crisis.*

Neither sentence is incomprehensible but there is a qualitative difference between them. One is somewhat clumsy, the other is focused. One says less but uses more words. The other says more but uses fewer words.

Each sentence you write is an opportunity for self-expression and self-representation. While writing for your degree, you will be writing assignments or essays containing informed commentary and involving the construction of propositions and arguments. These pieces of work are also opportunities for self-expression and self-representation. Tasks involving self-expression and self-representation have the potential to be daunting, if you are unaccustomed to them. They are also vehicles through which you can present yourself to the world, to your chosen course of study and to your profession. How you express yourself in writing is but another form of self-presentation, such as how you dress, how you convey your sense of style. So, just as these are important in terms of what they say about you, the same can be said for your written expression. Your approach is very important. The task of writing an assignment can be considered drudgery or an opportunity to step out in style. This is something you have to choose, but just as in other presentations of self, care, time and effort are involved if you are to be well presented, the same is true for your written expression. Few people are able to write well at the first draft. Amendment is more often involved with removing or changing words rather than adding them.

COMMENT

The main points in this section have been:

- *Your written expression is a form of personal presentation. How we write says something about ourselves, the care and clarity with which we express ourselves is an indication of how much we value such matters. Other values are also revealed: getting the names of people right and taking the trouble to report their wishes and feelings accurately when required says things about how we view, value and respect others, including service users.*

- *How you feel about the task is likely to colour your approach towards it. Your approach is important; assignment writing can be regarded as a chore or something in which you can take pride. Your approach is likely to be reflected in the quality of your work. Realistically you are likely to find some subjects a little harder-going in comparison with others but if you can recognise the value in knowing more about the topic and find an interesting aspect within it, writing about it will be less burdensome.*

Sentence construction

Sentences can be well crafted, concise and accurately reflect what you want to say. At the other end of the scale they can be so poor as to detract from the meaning the writer wishes to convey. Your writing skills play a part in the quality of your work but a little time and effort spent on checking that the sentences you have used comply with the following properties is time well spent.

It is possible to approach sentence construction in a very complicated way that involves clause analysis and an exacting application of grammar. The approach taken in this book will be more concerned with identifying what makes for well-constructed sentences that convey meaning accurately and concisely. However, there are some fundamental rules of English grammar that have to be understood and complied with even when taking this less esoteric approach to sentence construction. The main rule is concerned with what constitutes a sentence. A sentence is a group of words that makes complete sense and, when written, begins with a capital letter and ends with a full stop, or an exclamation or question mark. Grammatically correct sentences usually contain a main verb and a noun or pronoun but there can be exceptions to this, most often permissible in informal writing or written dialogue.

A verb is a word that describes an action of some kind. Verbs are also described as 'doing' words. Examples include:

carry

defend

entertain

frighten

Nouns are naming words. They may include the names of people or things. Examples may include:

carriage

defendant

entertainment

fright

Peter

Pronouns include I, you, he, she, it, we and they and may take the place of nouns that have already been used. For example: 'Peter went to the shop. He spent all his pocket money.'

Sentences that contain a verb and a noun pass the first test of what most commonly constitutes a sentence but their presence alone does not make for a grammatically correct, well-constructed sentence. Such sentences also have to have certain properties. The main one is an ability to make sense when the sentence is read alone, outside of the text in which it lies. The number of words in a sentence is not a criterion for what constitutes a sentence but another property of a well-written sentence is that it should not be longer than necessary in order to convey its meaning.

By applying the rule and the properties it is possible to recognise the words 'Jesus wept' as a grammatically correct sentence. 'Jesus' is the noun, being a naming word, whereas 'wept' is the verb as it describes an action. It makes sense when read alone, away from the rest of the text. Although only two words are used, no more are needed to convey its meaning. Compare that with 'The defendant lowered his head'. By applying the rule and properties this too is a grammatically correct, well-constructed sentence. 'Defendant' is the noun and 'lowered' is the verb. It makes sense and does not contain unused or unnecessary words to convey its meaning. The sentence could be added to: 'The defendant lowered his head as the charge was read out'. This still complies with the rule and properties of sentence construction but consider if 'as the charge was read out' was presented as a separate sentence. There is a verb, 'read', and a noun, 'charge'. So this sentence complies with the rule but not the property of making sense when read alone and is therefore not grammatically correct. Although this may seem elementary, grammatically incorrect and poorly constructed sentences do occur in presented work. A thorough proof reading of your work should identify them, allowing for their correction prior to submission.

Consider the following sentences and decide if they are well written or not, and if not, why not?

Sentence 1: This is in order to coincide with the common assessment framework and also the five outcomes of Every Child Matters.

Sentence 2: It will be discussed if emotional abuse has an impact on the child's psychological and physical development.

The first sentence fails to comply with the property of making sense when read outside of any text in which it occurs. The reader is prompted to ask; what does 'this' refer to, what had been done 'in order' to …?

The second sentence complies with the rules of sentence construction but the order in which the words appear is clumsy and could be improved:

The impact of emotional abuse on the child's psychological and physical development will be discussed.

COMMENT

It is difficult to construct sentences that do not contain either a noun or a verb; try it for yourself. In academic writing, as opposed to more informal prose such as diary entries or written dialogue, most sentences will contain a noun and a verb. It is easier to construct badly written sentences but to construct a sentence without a noun, pronoun or a verb is difficult without naming something about which you want to say something and go on to say what it was that happened to that person or thing, which is, of course, another way of describing the role of a noun and a verb. A good way of checking if a sentence is well constructed is to read it aloud; it should make sense both within and apart from the text in which it occurs.

The use of 'but' and 'and'

Avoid using 'but' and 'and' to start sentences. 'But' and 'and' are joining words and as such their use to start sentences is not recommended as the 'property condition' of a good sentence, making sense on its own, is more difficult to achieve. The use of conjunctives (as they are called) is usually reserved for written dialogue, although 'however' may be used to illustrate the counter position. For example: The words 'and' and 'but' are joining words and as such should not be used to start a sentence. However, their use is permitted when writing down and reporting dialogue.

Punctuation

This section will concentrate on the use of punctuation that tends to cause particular problems for students, rather than detail how all punctuation is used. You may find slight variation in other texts on the use of punctuation but for general use the following advice is sound.

The **full stop** is used to denote the end of a sentence mainly but is also used to indicate an abbreviation.

Capital letters are used: at the beginning of a new sentence; for proper nouns (names of people and places); for any titles of documents, books, publications, etc. Include the first letter of the first word and those of any significant words contained in the title, e.g.: *The Framework for the Assessment of Children in Need and their Families*.

The **question mark** should be used for all direct questions, e.g.: *Do you think that is the correct usage?*

The **comma** is used to denote a natural pause within a sentence. It is also used to make the writer's meaning clear and make complex sentences easier to read, e.g.: *I like everyone else have my own value base*. Here the writer appears to say that they like everyone else, but the meaning they want to convey goes on to be confused. The writer's meaning becomes clear when the commas are added: *I, like everyone else, have my own value base*.

The **comma** can also be used to separate words in a list, e.g.: *Attachment styles are categorised into secure, ambivalent, avoidant and disorganised attachments*. To separate longer and more complex lists a semi-colon should be used (see semi-colon).

The **comma** should also be used either side of a qualifying insertion, e.g.: *The welfare of children, in England and Wales, is primarily legislated for through the Children Act 1989*.

Single **quotation marks** (also called inverted commas) are used to highlight text or to put words in parenthesis, e.g.: *Childhood is considered a period of 'vulnerability' in comparison with that of adulthood*.

Double quotation marks should be used to indicate a direct quote (either a written or a verbal quotation), e.g.: *Lord Laming found the child protection system to be "basically sound"*.

The use of the **apostrophe** can cause difficulty but it is important and cannot be dispensed with as it can convey quite different meanings.

Firstly, it conveys ownership, e.g.: *The children's climbing frame was in the garden*. It is the climbing frame belonging to the children.

Secondly, it indicates if we are talking about one, or many, as these two examples make clear.

1. *None of the car's windows remained intact in the accident.*

2. *None of the cars' windows remained intact in the accident.*

In the first sentence the way the apostrophe is used denotes that only one car had its windows broken, whereas in the second sentence all the cars involved in the accident had their windows broken.

A common error in the use of the apostrophe is adding one when it is not needed, e.g.: *The number of public house's closing in England has exceeded ten per week*. The use of an apostrophe here is incorrect as all that is required is the plural, i.e., *houses*.

Thirdly, the apostrophe replaces the missing letter when words are shortened. These are called contractions, e.g.: do not becomes *don't*, that is becomes *that's*. However, contractions should not be used in academic writing.

The final two punctuation marks you need to be able to use are the **colon** (:) and the **semi-colon** (;). A colon is used to introduce a list or an explanation. A semi-colon is used to separate the items in a list and to divide a complex sentence where the two parts are linked, e.g.:

There are several orders that may be applied for under parts IV and V of the Children Act 1989: interim care orders; full care orders; interim supervision orders; supervision orders; child assessment orders; emergency protection orders.

The threshold test for whether or not a court would consider making any of these orders is broadly the same; it turns on whether or not there are reasonable grounds for suspecting or believing the child concerned is suffering or is likely to suffer significant harm.

The importance of the appropriate use of punctuation and the contribution such usage makes to presentation and clarity of meaning cannot be overemphasised.

ACTIVITY **1.4**

Compare the following unpunctuated paragraph:

childcare social workers need to have an understanding of child development as an important part of their role is to undertake assessments of childrens developmental needs they are not solely responsible for determining this however they need to have a level of knowledge that would alert them to a child who had additional needs or a child in need as defined under s17 of the children act 1989 or a child in need of safeguarding are social workers expected to come to such decisions based entirely on their own assessments no but they would be expected to know when it would be appropriate to consult a health visitor or a paediatrician who will have specialist knowledge in their respective roles in order to better inform their assessment mary sheridans charts laying out childrens developmental milestones are a useful source of information for social workers as they explain what children should be capable of at what age health visitors should be fully conversant with these charts as they routinely undertake developmental assessments

with this correctly punctuated paragraph:

Childcare social workers need to have an understanding of child development as an important part of their role is to undertake assessments of children's developmental needs. They are not solely responsible for determining this; however, they need to have a level of knowledge that would alert them to a child who had additional needs, or a 'child in need' as defined under s17 of the Children Act 1989, or a child in need of safeguarding. Are social workers expected to come to such decisions based entirely on their own assessments? No, but they would be expected to know when it would be appropriate to consult a health visitor or a paediatrician, who will have specialist knowledge in their respective roles, in order to better inform their assessment. Mary Sheridan's charts laying out children's developmental milestones are a useful source of information for social workers, as they explain what children should be capable of at what age. Health Visitors should be fully conversant with these charts as they routinely undertake developmental assessments.

Continued

Did you agree with the punctuation? If you are unsure about how to use punctuation correctly, then now is the time to sort it out so you can then go on to write with confidence and fluidity. In addition to punctuating the paragraph I also 'justified' it to remove the ragged edge, a facility in the tool bar usually on the right hand side, as this improves presentation.

Spelling

Spelling words and people's names correctly is important. Failure to do so will result in your losing marks and, depending on the extent, suggest to the reader that you have a sloppy approach to the craft of written communication. Spelling people's names accurately conveys to the reader that doing so matters to you and, in consequence, you are demonstrating respect for the person concerned. This is important for your service users as well as authors you may refer to. Spell-checking programs go some way to identifying errors but they cannot be relied upon totally as some words can be spelt correctly but used incorrectly, e.g.: *The buoy went too the counter two ask the thyme of the train but was told he had mist it*. A rather implausible sentence admittedly but the point is the spell-checking program failed to identify any one of the five spelling errors contained in the sentence. A proof read is not solely for content but for spelling also. You have options as to which form of English you can use for your spell-check program. Use UK English and not US English as a number of words in American English may replace the letter 's' with a 'z' and the ending 'our' with 'or' and as a result will be spelt incorrectly.

Paragraphs, subheadings and bullet points

The use of paragraphs

Paragraphs are used to break up dense blocks of text. These breaks should occur at points where the writer is moving to a new topic within the context of the piece or addressing a different aspect of the same topic to the one explored in the previous paragraph.

Paragraphs are denoted by either a new line with an indentation or a complete line break. They are important to the structure of your work and each should end with a concluding comment before starting the new paragraph with a new topic, idea or development of the overall argument. The length of the paragraph is dictated by the content but a minimum would be three or four sentences and a maximum could take up most of the page, but a page of A4 should contain at least one new paragraph. Complex paragraphs may be thought of as mini assignments in themselves, with an introduction, main body and concluding comments.

The use of subheadings

Using subheadings can improve the structure and coherence of your work. However, it is important to establish the format of the piece of work you have been asked to undertake. Descriptions may include an essay, an assignment or a report. In academic convention an essay does not usually contain subheadings, assignments may contain subheadings and reports usually do, but you need to check with the particular tutor you are writing the piece of work for whether the inclusion of subheadings is acceptable.

Unless you are an experienced writer it is recommended that you write using subheadings. If their presence is not acceptable you can remove them from the draft prior to submission. Page 4 in this chapter contains a comment about specific assessment criteria or learning outcomes that you may be expected to explicitly address as part of your response to the assessment task you have been asked to undertake. Where this is so, use these criteria for your subheadings as doing so will increase the likelihood of you writing a specific, contained and focused response.

The use of bullet points

Bullet points are a useful way of presenting information in a concise manner. Bullet-point text needs to be:

- short;

- self-explanatory;

- focused;

- used sparingly;

- relevant to the text above and below their inclusion.

Bullet points tend to be best used in electronic presentations such as PowerPoint where the presenter should verbally develop the points. They may be appropriately used in reports and portfolios but check with the tutor you are writing for whether their use is acceptable in essays and assignments.

Have you addressed the question in the manner required?

You would be surprised at the number of pieces of work that, despite being grammatically well written, are failed because the student concerned has not addressed the question or in the manner required. Despite the development of tutors' offering briefing sessions on the assignment task this problem remains.

Be clear about what is required for the assessment before you start work on it and if in doubt, ask for clarification.

Below is a list of common words used in assignment tasks. You need to have an accurate understanding of what these words mean.

Describe … say what something is and how it works

Many students receive critical feedback saying that their work is too descriptive. It is often necessary to describe the context in which what you are writing about takes place but this may be brief and care should be taken that descriptive accounts do not contain unnecessary information, often called 'padding' and 'waffle'.

Comment on … give an opinion

It is usually expected that this is an 'informed' opinion, informed by reading around the topic. You may be expected to cite other opinions, or substantiate yours by referring to authors. If so you will need to give an 'in text' reference and include a full reference in your reference list. Where your opinion is not qualified with reference to source material and is simply your view, you need to make this clear to the reader.

Compare ... Identify similarities

Contrast ... Identify differences

Assignment tasks sometimes ask you to 'compare and contrast ...'. It is important that you do both.

Analyse ... goes further than description to say what is going on in order to understand and explain it

Discuss ... Debate the arguments for and against a particular position

Define ... This requires a precise, short, unequivocal statement about what something is. Often a dictionary sourced definition may be appropriate

Explain ... or *Offer an explanation of* ... this should address the how, why, when and where of the issue

Evaluate ... How good is it? How effective is this idea, this intervention?

Critically appraise ... builds on an analysis of something to make judgements about its efficacy

Writing critically is a particular skill you will develop during your course of study. It is more than finding fault with something. It is offering informed comment on a particular issue in a way that amounts to an evaluation of how useful an idea or thing is, or the extent to which it offers an explanation of a particular phenomenon; it involves coming to a *decision*. For example, Sigmund Freud had some very interesting ideas about what lay behind certain family dynamics and relationships. A critical appraisal of this would offer an informed opinion or an evaluation of the contribution his theories have made to an understanding of family relationships and the contribution his ideas have made to our knowledge of the human condition. To be 'informed' it must be more than just one person's viewpoint. It may be informed through a review of his research methodology, and authoritative commentary from his supporters and detractors. This is the way the *argument* would be reasoned but ultimately a conclusion would be reached. For example: Freud's theories on psychosexual development remain controversial. However, the importance of his role in promoting the idea that the child's psyche is a topic worthy of study cannot be denied.

Review ... Undertake a survey (of literature, for example)

Summarise ... Write a short account of the main points

This is not an exhaustive list of all the words you will come across in assignment questions. The important point is that you have a clear, accurate understanding of what you are being asked to do.

Using quotations and paraphrasing

When quoting from an author you must make an exact copy of the original with quotation marks (") either side of the quote, followed by an in-text reference and a full reference in the reference list. You are advised to use quotations sparingly and they should only be two or three sentences long. For example:

> *"As with symbolic communication, social workers need to be aware of how they use non-verbal behaviour, including facial expression, gaze, orientation and body movement and its potential meaning for users of services."*
>
> Lishman (2009, page 32)

For the in-text reference you are required to put the page number on which the quote appears in the original source. The full reference in the reference list would be:

Lishman, J (2009) *Communication in Social Work*. Basingstoke: Palgrave Macmillan.

Paraphrasing

This is when you reflect back what an author has said but in your own words. For example:

> *Social workers should be aware of what their body language is saying to their service users.*
>
> (Lishman 2009).

There is still an in text reference given in order to attribute the sentiment to the original source but no page number is needed. The full reference needs to be written in the reference list in the same way as before.

How much should you read or reference and what ratio of books to journals to e-sources should be used?

Your tutor or the institution where you are studying may have views on this and should be consulted.

How much you should read and reference cannot be easily quantified as there is a qualitative dimension to the extent to which your source material informs your work. However, for a general idea, 6–12 independent references constitute a reasonable number for a 2000–2500-word assignment. However, this might be considered a minimum if this includes background reading material as well as in-text cited references. Between 12 and 18 independent references with a high level of relevant in-text citation are likely to constitute a well-researched assignment. Avoid writing a long list of references in your reference list or bibliography but having only a few in-text references. Make sure you have included the full reference details in the list for every reference you have referred to in your text.

The ratio of books to journals to e-sources is not specified as this too is not easily quantified, but for a general idea apply 3:2:1. E-books in this context may be regarded as books.

Remember, the purpose of referencing is twofold: firstly it is to attribute the source of your information to the original author and, secondly, to allow your reader to find your source material either to read more of the original or to validate your use of it. You therefore need to avoid unattributed articles, e-sources or those that cannot be returned to. You also need to give the date when you accessed the site in the reference. The accuracy of the information contained in Wikis cannot be guaranteed because anyone can add information to these, so use with caution if at all.

Assertion and supporting your comments (substantiation)

An assertion is a statement presented as a fact, for example: *The UK is overpopulated*. Assertions are often opinions but presented as undisputed facts, unless the writer makes it clear: *In my opinion, the UK is overpopulated*. In this second sentence you know that this assertion is the writer's opinion and, by inference, the writer is acknowledging that this is disputable as other opinions may exist.

An unsupported assertion is one without any supporting evidence. An unqualified assertion is one that is presented as a fact; it becomes qualified when prefixed with 'in my opinion' or 'it could be argued that …'. There is a place for unsupported and unqualified assertion: for example, newspapers often lead their articles with headline-grabbing assertions. It is, however, considered poor scholarly practice when writing academically. The objective when writing academically is to represent whatever is being written about in an objective way, rather than in an opinionated way, and to accurately reveal the complexity of the issue being considered. So, bringing an academic way of writing to our example, reference would have to be made to questions such as: how would we know when a country was overpopulated and what criteria could be relied upon and applied to determine whether a county was overpopulated? Could we use the ratio of the area of land to the number of people populating it? Could we use whether or not a country can grow sufficient food to feed its population, or can fully employ or house or provide health care for its population? These questions would have to be considered against inter-country trade in food, emigration and immigration. We would have to consider the fact that there are examples of small countries with large numbers of people whose needs are reasonably well met and ones where they are poorly met. You can see why writing academically is challenging!

Here is an other example, linked to social work: *About 10% of communication is verbal*. This sentence is academically poor: it is an unsupported, unqualified assertion and there is insufficient information to be meaningful. Does it relate to *all* communication? What about a tape recording? Now consider this sentence: *It is a widely accepted belief in professional circles that about 80% of our communication is non-verbal*. This sentence is a little better: it is a partially qualified assertion, qualified by stating that it is 'widely accepted' in 'professional circles' but it is woolly and would be marked down for its lack of specificity in respect of how wide is 'widely' and which 'professional circles' are involved? To what extent do they validate the statement? Now consider this statement:

> *What we say only contributes a small proportion to what is exchanged in our interpersonal communication. Darn suggests that less than 10% of interpersonal communication involves words; he identifies the role of voice tone, body language, touch, eye contact and defensible space as being more significant in communication.*
>
> Darn (2005)

And in the reference list:

Darn, S (2005) 'Aspects of nonverbal communication' *Internet TESL journal* XI (2) [online]. Available from: http://iteslj.org/Articles/Darn-Nonverbal/ [accessed 18/10/2010].

This statement is much better: it is qualified and supported and provides the reader with a coherent piece of information.

Avoid quoting from lecture slides unless the source is referenced on the slide and you can replicate this. Lecture slides represent summarised information that often requires expanding on through your research of source materials. They are best thought of as guidance as to where to start to direct your reading.

Writing in the third person

It is an important academic convention that written work is usually presented in the third person. There may be occasions, however, where it will be acceptable or even required to write in the first person. An example of this could be writing reflectively and from personal experience, for example:

During my practice placement I had direct experience of working with women who had experienced domestic abuse. Initially I could not understand why these women remained with their abusive partners but after I had listened to their stories, I began to appreciate some of the significant issues that made it difficult to leave and influenced their reasons to try to maintain their relationships.

However, the use of 'I' (first person singular), 'we' (first person plural) or 'you' (second person) in written assignments should generally be avoided. Errors in this are often made at the beginning of assignments, for example:

In this assignment I will look at the impact living with domestic abuse has on child development.

Or use of the first person plural:

In this assignment we will think about the impact of domestic abuse on child development.

Or use of the second person:

In this assignment you will see how living with domestic abuse has an impact on child development.

The beginning of an introduction that complies with the academic convention would be:

This assignment will consider the impact of domestic violence on child development.

Plagiarism

Plagiarism constitutes an academic offence. It is important that you understand what this is and that you avoid it. The following case studies give examples of two common types of plagiarism.

CASE STUDY

Alison is a mature student who felt somewhat daunted coming to study for her degree because it has been a long time since she has undertaken any type of formal learning. She attended her induction week which was packed with information, some of which she felt went over her head. There was such a lot to take in and, as she lacked confidence, she was reluctant to seek clarification on some issues she was unclear about.

She has recently submitted her first assignment on values and ethics but was alarmed to learn in her feedback that not only had she failed with a mark of 20% but was under investigation for an allegation of plagiarism.

Her tutor had marked her work and suspected that some sections had been copied from a text without any author being attributed. He had run it through a computer software program that helps detect plagiarism. It produced a correlation of 70%, confirming his suspicions which led to the allegation and investigation.

Alison had included several paragraphs of text from a book in her work but had not made any reference that she had done so. Alison had reasoned that the author explained it so much better than she could and was unaware that what she had done constituted an academic offence as she did not really understand plagiarism. As she was in her first year, she was interviewed by the head of school, who advised her that she would need to resubmit her assignment and warned her that if there was another incidence of plagiarism she could lose her place on the course.

Alison felt embarrassed and annoyed with herself for not having understood or having bothered to find out what plagiarism was, but knew ignorance was no excuse. She remembered it being talked about during induction week.

CASE STUDY

Martin was in the second year of his degree. He had struggled with his academic work during the first year and had not settled well into the halls of residence as he initially missed his family and friends. Things had taken a turn for the better towards the end of the first year when he started seeing a girlfriend but she had been the victim of a road traffic accident and had been in hospital and Martin had been visiting on a regular basis. He had not sought any support in dealing with these issues, which had seriously disrupted his studies. He had been due to submit his assignment on child development but had missed a couple of the lectures and had hardly done any reading or work on the assignment. He panicked and wondered what to do. He was friendly with Sue, who he considered an able, well-organised student. He asked to see her assignment, just to compare it with his. Sue sent him a copy and he thought that by altering it a little by rearranging the order of some of the words and adding some of his own, he could submit it as his own work and his immediate problems would be resolved.

The tutor noticed the similarity of the two scripts but was uncertain who had copied from whom, though he had his suspicions. Both Martin and Sue were subject to an

Continued

CASE STUDY *continued*

allegation of an academic offence and were interviewed by the head of year tutor and head of school. Martin admitted copying Sue's work and submitting it as his without her knowledge. Sue remained on the course, her record unblemished, but she was upset at what Martin had done. Martin had to await the decision of a disciplinary panel; he was in danger of losing his place on the course. There was the issue of plagiarism but also dishonesty, contravening the General Social Care Council's Codes of Practice, which student social workers and qualified social workers agree to abide by.

COMMENT

Tutors see a lot of work and are often capable of identifying academic offences. Students do sometimes find themselves in difficulties with respect to time management issues but taking the shortcuts described in the case studies is not a solution. It is far better for the student to speak to someone in order to receive support and have submission dates rescheduled than to cheat, risk being 'found out' and sullying their reputation, potentially jeopardising their place on the course and damaging their employment prospects.

Presentation and preparing your work for submission

There is usually a module handbook or module descriptor made available to you that will describe the assignment task and other important requirements regarding presentation. Read this and comply with what is required.

Write in the font style, size and line spacing required. Keep within 10 per cent either way of the word limit, unless you are required to do otherwise write within the stipulated length.

Use the tool bar options to number your pages, provide a word count and justify word alignment. This icon is on the right hand side of the alignment options and aligns the words in neat blocks of text resulting in an even edge on both left and right hand sides. Include a title and a means of identification – this will be your name or just your student number if your institution uses an anonymous submission procedure. Remember always to keep a 'back up' copy of the piece of work you are submitting.

Address the essay question or assignment task in a logical sequence, with an introduction that is then developed in the main body and a conclusion. Try to keep your sentences short, use paragraphs and sub-headings (if this is permitted) to help the structure, focus and organisation of your work.

Include a reference list that complies with the rules for reference lists or bibliographies specified by your institution. You may simply have to learn this by rote and this can be somewhat tedious, but, getting it right is much less tedious than still being corrected and losing marks for referencing errors in your final year!

Understand what constitutes an academic offence and avoid being accused of this; it is an embarrassing process and unnecessary.

You might feel, upon or near a piece of work's completion, that you do not want to spend any more time on it and just want to submit it, but it is vital that the work is proof read prior to submission: your work deserves it! Proof reading is a way to identify and correct grammatical, typographical and spelling errors. Initially subject your work to the spelling and grammar check program on your computer, but you cannot solely rely on this for reasons already explained in this chapter, so read your work through again. Does it 'make sense'? Does it reflect what you want to say? Does it address the set question or assignment task? If possible ask someone else to read it; they do not need to be someone studying the same subject, in fact it is better that they are not. Does it 'make sense' to them? Read the work aloud to yourself in accord with the way you have punctuated it. Poorly constructed sentences stand out when heard as they do not comply with the 'making sense alone' rule.

Only when you have done this and corrected the errors found is your work ready to submit.

Using feedback from previous assignments

If you are satisfied (or even disappointed) with the mark a piece of work has achieved, there is a temptation to just put it to one side and not properly reflect on the tutor's comments. If you do this it is a learning opportunity lost. It is very important that you understand the reasons why the work merited the mark it achieved, especially if you were disappointed and crucially if the work did not achieve a pass as you will need to re-submit the assignment and you will need to know what you need to do to achieve a pass. If this is not clear to you, or if the comments are illegible or confusing or incongruent with the mark, seek clarification from the marker. Feedback should contain the rationale for the mark awarded, it should identify strengths and areas where you could have improved the work and hence the mark. Act on the latter point by incorporating advice and suggestions into the next piece of work.

CHAPTER SUMMARY

This chapter has introduced some fundamental concepts about writing well for university. It started with acknowledging the importance of motivation in writing well. It then identified the skills required to write successfully at university, including the ability to: write in an academic style; comprehend competing theories of explanation and argument; find, use and attribute a range of source material.

The skills audit provided you with an opportunity to self-assess your current level of ability in the skills required. Any shortfall should be addressed through an action plan.

This was followed with information that would help you to achieve a good standard of written English which included:

- sentence construction;
- punctuation and spelling;
- paragraphs, sub-headings and bullet points;
- understanding the assignment task;   *Continued*

CHAPTER SUMMARY continued

- using quotations and paraphrasing;

- assertion and supported commentary;

- writing in the third person;

- plagiarism;

- presentation;

- using feedback.

Understanding each of these points and applying them in your writing will enable you to write well for university. Please remember, however, that the use of personal pronouns such as 'I', 'my', 'we' and 'our', of subheadings, of internet references and the rules of exactly how to apply a referencing system may all be subject to slight variation according to the tutor or the academic institution you are attending, so do ensure you are complying with what is required. As you will go on to see in the following chapters on placement preparation and writing for practice, these skills are generic to writing well in a professional context as well as academically, and they can be transferred to writing for practice placements and post-qualifying practice.

FURTHER READING

The following books on studying and study skills are additional sources of information on how to further develop your writing skills.

Cotterell, S (2004) *The study skills handbook.* 2nd edition. Basingstoke: Palgrave.

Stella Cotterell's book is a comprehensive guide to study skills and contains many useful ideas on, for example, methods you can employ to help organise your thoughts and structure your assignment.

Northedge, A (2005) *The good study guide.* 2nd edition. Buckingham: Open University Press.

Andrew Northedge's book systematically considers the presentation of information in academic writing. He stresses the importance of writing well and provides many developmental examples of how to present your work to a high standard.

Peck, J and Coyle, M (eds.) (2005) *Write it right: A handbook for students.* Basingstoke: Palgrave.

John Peck and Martin Coyle's book concentrates on the skills needed to write to a good standard of expression. Specific emphasis is placed on the use of grammar, punctuation and spelling.

Walker, H (2011) *Studying for your social work degree.* 2nd edition. Exeter: Learning Matters.

Hilary Walker's book is specifically orientated toward the study skills required to study for a degree in social work. While this includes many generic skills, the book is very helpful in the aspects of occupational application of key skills such as reflection in practice.

Chapter 2

Placement preparation and practice

Introduction

Before the skills required for writing for practice placements can be considered there are a number of issues regarding practice placements that need to be discussed. What follows is written in respect of assessed placements, as opposed to brief non-assessed placements, which tend to be observational in nature.

Assessed placements are subject to various levels of scrutiny: the student's practice is assessed by the practice educator (aka practice teacher or assessor); the quality of the placement as a learning experience is assessed by the General Social Care Council; the course within which placements are offered is assessed by the awarding body so placements occur within a stratified regulatory framework. The purpose of undertaking practice placements is essentially two-fold: firstly the course has to offer you experience of practice so that you may develop your craft and apply your learning at university to a practice setting, secondly it has to create the opportunity for you to demonstrate competence in the given occupational requirements that apply. Currently these are the National Occupational Standards (NOS) and include specified Values Requirements (VR). Equally important to the occupational standards are the 'benchmark statements' for social work specified by the Quality Assurance Agency. The professional requirements contained in the benchmarking statements are incorporated into the structure of your university course. On placement you will be assessed against the NOS and VR. Nevertheless, it is important for you to understand the knowledge skills and values you are expected to acquire during your course of learning from both these sources; accordingly they are reproduced in Appendices 1 and 2 at the end of this book.

It is the present government's stated intention to abolish the GSCC in 2012 and transfer its functions to the Health Professions Council, whose name will be changed to reflect this. Change is a characteristic feature of any dynamic profession and this one is an important development for social work. However, the NOS, or their equivalent, will endure irrespective of which body heads them and students will be assessed against these on placement. Another important document you need to be aware of is the GSCC's Codes of Practice. The codes are a set of ethical principles that student and qualified social workers must comply with in order to gain and retain their registration. The codes also include what social care employers should provide for their employees and you are advised to familiarise yourself with these in order to know what you are entitled to. However, in practice placements you will need to demonstrate that your practice complies with the codes relevant for practitioners. A copy of the codes for social care employees is reproduced in Appendix 3 at the end of this book.

The NOS and VR, the benchmark statements and Codes of Practice provide the structure for the knowledge, skills and values you will be expected to demonstrate on placement. You will need to demonstrate competence in all aspects of the six key roles of the NOS over the course of your placements. These 'key roles' are specified and must be addressed. However, the exact detail of the way in which the other components should be incorporated into courses and the practice portfolio was not specified by the regulatory, quality assurance and awarding bodies. This has meant that Higher Education Institutions (HEIs) offering qualifying social work courses have, to some extent, designed their own courses, within certain specified parameters such as the NOS and the (total) number of days in practice placements, currently 200. Thereafter HEIs have largely decided for themselves how those 200 days should be divided over how many placements, with each addressing specified key roles (KR). For example:

- University 'A' might specify that on their course there are two 100-day placements, in each of the second and third years. The first placement will address KR 1, 3 and 5 whereas the second placement will address KR 2, 4 and 6.

- University 'B' might specify a 40-day placement in the first year which addresses KR 1, a 70-day placement in the second year that addresses KR 2 and 3 and a 90-day placement in the third year that addresses KR 4, 5 and 6.

There may be other universities offering different combinations of placement duration, addressing different combinations of key roles, or re-visiting some as the student nears professional qualification. The Social Work Task Force reported in 2009 on a number of proposed changes to the social work profession which included Recommendation 3: Improving the Quality of Practice Placements. In consequence, the Social Work Reform Board is proposing that the structure of placements is standardised to one placement of 70 days, another of 100 days with 30 days set aside for skills development (see the Social Work Reform Board's report *Building a safe and confident future: One year on,* 2010).

Does any of this matter? Yes and No is the answer. No, if you are concerned about the quality of your learning experience as each HEI, in offering a course, will have had its course quality assessed and approved by the GSCC or its replacement body. There may be arguments for and against certain combinations of placement curricula. For example, it may be useful to have an experience of social work practice early in your course through a short practice placement but you will not have had much theoretical input by then. Conversely, a longer placement after a greater amount of theoretical input could create the opportunity for a more 'in-depth' placement experience but the opportunity to experience social work practice is delayed. However, all courses will lead to professional qualification provided you pass the course, so 'in the round' it does not matter. The 'Yes' part of the answer is two-fold. The way the HEI organises its practice placements may be important to you, you may have even chosen your course on the basis of the way your HEI arranges its placements or you may have considered it a significant factor. It is also very important that you understand the placement arrangements and assessment requirements for your particular course. This will be described in the course literature, placement handbook or module specification. Do take the time to become familiar with it: the practice placements constitute a significant proportion of the 360 academic credits that make up an undergraduate degree and you have to pass practice placements to qualify, so understand the criteria you are being assessed against. You will also need to understand and act on what you need to do for your pre-placement preparation. There will be a number of processes and documents you will need to have in place before being able to undertake a placement. This will include your HEI's version of a 'Fitness to Practise assessment', which is a process the GSCC requires HEIs to successfully conduct with their students prior to and dependent upon commencing an assessed practice placement. Some HEIs include a short placement as part of this process. Students will also need to have a student registration with the GSCC and a satisfactory Criminal Records Bureau check so they can be approved to work with vulnerable people.

Placement choice and 'statutory' placements

Your practice placements are very important experiences. They are vital to your success as you need to 'pass' them but this is not the only manner in which they are important. They are, for many, a rich learning experience, remembered and reminisced upon over a practitioner's career. Many students will have seen examples of practice by a practitioner whose skill and ability they were impressed by and wanted to emulate. Some may have seen practice examples they considered other than 'good' and would not want to incorporate into their practice, but this too is a valuable learning experience. For many students, their placements may have influenced a career choice and may even have led to a job upon qualification. Whether you want to 'explore' some areas of social work practice or have a firm idea of a particular area of service provision or service user group you ultimately want to work in or with, it is worth thinking about possible placement opportunities. In any event it is far too important a learning opportunity to leave entirely to chance so think about the type of placement experience you are hoping for and in which area of social work practice.

The demand for placements is such that it is unlikely that you will be able to 'choose' your placement. It is more likely to be, at best, a negotiated process with your HEI's placement co-ordinator and dependent on a number of variables that may include local competition for placements and level of demand at the time for placement provision across the public, private and voluntary sectors and the availability of practice educators. Although these factors are not in your control it remains to your advantage to have thought about your learning needs in respect of your placement, with a caveat that you may not be offered your first choice.

Some placement co-ordinators attempt to provide their students with one 'statutory' placement from those their particular course offers which can complement a common expectation of students. It also has the potential to be a bone of contention if the student does not think they have been provided with the type of placement opportunities they are entitled to. There is a tendency to associate a placement within a local authority's children's services or adult services as being 'statutory' placements and, in consequence, providing a more demanding or higher-quality learning experience than that of placements in the private and voluntary sectors. This notion is simplistic and has the potential to be discriminatory to all non-local authority placements as offering a poorer learning experience, which is inaccurate. While it is important that students have the opportunity to undertake statutory work and work with involuntary clients, the mixed economy of service provision has meant that such work is no longer the preserve of local authorities; indeed many have commissioned private and voluntary organisations to undertake their statutory responsibilities on their behalf. For example, in Lincolnshire the charity Barnardo's provides the Leaving Care Service and fulfils the responsibilities that the Children (Leaving Care) Act 2000 confers on the local authority. It is far from the only example of 'outsourcing' and such initiatives look set to increase rather than diminish in future.

There are practical considerations regarding placements as well as anticipating whether the type of placement will meet your learning needs, for example the location of your placement.

Placement location

If you are attending university away from your 'home', do you want one or more of your placements in your 'home' locality? If you do, is this possible? Are there any issues you need to consider, such as if you are likely to know your service users or could they know you in another context? Can you get to the placement at the times you are required to be there? How do you feel about working in one place such as a residential setting, or a secure setting, or a hospital? If you have a fieldwork placement in a rural area you are likely to need independent transport. If you are expected to transport service users you will need 'business use' insurance as well as private use car insurance. These are just a few of the practical issues you may need to consider.

There are, at least potentially, some emotional issues you need to consider about placements. No amount of preparatory thinking or research could fully prepare you for the learning experience your placements will offer you, nor should it, but it is possible to anticipate some situations and it is worthwhile doing so. For example: If you or someone close to you had been a victim of domestic abuse, how would you feel about a placement with Women's Aid? Or, if your grandfather or grandmother's health is deteriorating or if they are dying how would you feel about a placement in a home for the elderly? How do you feel about the people you are expecting to work with? Personal closeness to such issues should not, in itself, prevent you from seeking placements likely to further expose you to them, but a sound practitioner would consider the likely effect such issues may have and in what way. Social work is an emotionally demanding occupation in which indifference to another's plight is not an ethical option, not even for one's own protection. A worker who is emotionally unaffected by their contact with service users is likely to be ineffective as a social worker, as the quality of the working relationship is a determining factor in achieving desired outcomes. However, for the sake of one's own well-being it is important to be aware of the emotional impact the work is having and at what cost to the practitioner.

It is both understandable and reasonable for you to find yourself feeling scared, ignorant, de-skilled, challenged and powerless in response to some situations experienced for the first time on placements. The important thing is how you respond to these feelings and what you learn from having had them. It would be difficult to select one attribute above all others that could be considered essential for social workers to have, but if one had to, emotional intelligence would be a strong contender. An ability to glean a practical understanding of what is going on for your service user and yourself, both at apparent and emotionally underpinning levels, is a core skill and a key component of the 'professional competence' your practice educator is looking for evidence of you beginning to develop, or developing further, during the placement.

Your presentation on placement

The GSCC's Codes of Practice describe the expectations regarding your conduct, but as there is no 'dress code' you also need to think about your presentation. Social work is not, generally, considered a suit and tie or dressy blouse type of job unless you are in the court arena so casual dress is usually acceptable, but 'smart casual' is preferred to 'sloppy casual'. Social workers need to be sensitive to what their choice of dress is saying to their service user; this can be suggestive of power and authority but can include other messages, that though not intended could be open to misinterpretation, some of which may be conveyed through the choice of clothes or certain brand logos written on T-shirts, some of which merit consideration as to their appropriateness.

Establishing and maintaining professional boundaries

The relationship between the social worker and the person or people receiving the service is a complex one. Sometimes the person you are working *for*, your 'primary client', is not the person you are working *with*. This person might be the carer or parent of your primary client; a person with dementia or a child. You are not in the role of a friend in the same sense as a 'pal' to the person you are working with, yet you are rooting for them. You are seeking to help create an environment in which they can empower themselves to achieve a better outcome yet you must avoid appearing paternalistic. You are a representative of authority and power whilst seeking to dilute this and encourage participation and partnership. Essentially you are accompanying someone who is or is perceived to be 'vulnerable' on part, often a small part, of their journey in the capacity of a caring, helpful professional whose knowledge skills and values are being used to benefit the person receiving the service. The channel in which this can be successfully achieved is broad but there are rocks and sandbanks upon which one's professional integrity can be compromised.

Bearing witness to aspects of your service user's journey can be painful and feeling compassion may be unavoidable and entirely appropriate for the situation. Verbally acknowledging this may be appropriate but offer any physical gesture of comfort with caution and avoid such gestures that could be open to misinterpretation. You may come across situations where you are tempted to use your own money to alleviate a problem or offer to make yourself available 24/7 by giving a personal phone number or address, or offering contact 'outside' of work time, but these actions should be resisted as they 'cross' the boundary of what constitutes a professional relationship.

The advent of social networking sites can pose problems for establishing and maintaining professional integrity. Any information you upload on such sites may not be limited to your 'friends' but could 'go global' so consider the extent to which you can control the distribution of information and the nature of the information you are 'sharing'. This is also true for any personal disclosure you may feel is appropriate to share with the person with whom you are working. Being offered a gift or something that may be intended or perceived as such in appreciation of your work can also be problematical and advice and any protocol on how to respond to this and some of the other issues discussed in this paragraph are likely to be found in your agency's policy on staff conduct.

Practice placement opportunities

Social work is undertaken in a wide variety of contexts with people representing all aspects of life stage development from neo-natal wards to hospices. What follows is not an exhaustive list of possible placement settings and career opportunities but it will provide an idea of the scope.

Historically the provision of social services was arranged in a variety of structures such as generic or patch but, following specialisation, provision is usually divided into two service areas: services for children and services for adults. Although this arrangement is a generalisation, placement settings tend to reflect this division.

Placements where the primary service user is a child or young person
- *Family support.* Services are usually provided by the local authority, the private and voluntary sector. For example, family centres, local authority strengthening families or family support teams, Sure Start.

- *Children in public care and children leaving care.* Services are usually provided by the local authority and private, independent practice communities and voluntary organisations such as Barnardo's.

- *Children in adoptive care, foster care, children's homes, therapeutic communities and specialist educational placements.* Services are provided by the local authority, private and voluntary sectors, for example, Independent Fostering Association.

- *Children in the secure estate, at risk of offending, misusing substances, homelessness.* Services are usually provided by Young Offenders Institutions and secure units under the Home Office, local authority Youth Offending Teams, private and voluntary organisations such as NACRO, Sova, Turning Point, Addaction and housing associations.

- *Children who are ill or with physical disabilities and children with learning disabilities.* Services are usually provided by the local authority, area health authority, private and voluntary providers, for example, National Children's Homes. Placements could be in a range of settings: hospitals, specialist residential, respite and day care provision.

- *Children in need of safeguarding, children subject to legal dispute.* Services are provided by statutory agencies, placements could be with local authority Children's Services, Social Care, CAFCASS (Children and Family Court Advisory Support Service).

- *Children and young people with behavioural difficulties, including underachievement at school, mental health difficulties, high risk behaviour and self harm.* Services have a range of providers, from health and local authorities, the voluntary and private sector. Placements could be in schools, with Child and Adolescent Mental Health Services (CAMHS) and GP surgeries and specialist clinics.

Placements where the primary service user is an adult

- *Mental health.* Service provision is through local authority mental health teams and some private and voluntary provision, e.g. Mind.

- *Physical and learning disability.* Specifically dedicated teams for the provision of services are maintained by local authorities. There are private and voluntary services, often specialising in the specific condition, syndrome or type of accident or event that preceded the disability or impairment. For example, SCOPE, or the Stroke Association. Placement opportunities could include day and respite care, adult placement, transitions to or towards greater levels of independent living and transitions increasing levels of dependency.

- *Sensory impairment.* Provision of services is from a mixed economy. There are some dedicated services provided by the local authority but some private and voluntary provision such as Guide Dogs for the Blind and SENSE.

- *Hospital-based social work.* There are hospital-based social work teams dedicated to work with particular groups of patients. Social workers are often involved in transitions from hospital into the community. As with physical and learning disability there are many private and voluntary organisations involved in supporting patients and who are knowledgeable about the condition or illness concerned.

- *Elderly and geriatric care, palliative care (community-based).* There are local authority dedicated teams that support this service user group in the community, arranging day, respite and residential care. The hospice movement is a significant charitable provider of end of life care.

- *Resettlement and rehabilitation of offenders, homelessness.* Much of the work with offenders and the transition to the community on their release is undertaken by the Probation Service, but there can be a role for social workers in certain situations. NACRO are a significant independent service provider in this area. There are a number of organisations that provide short-term accommodation, such as Hostels for the Homeless and the Nomad Trust.

- *Community support.* There are a whole range of community-based support and development projects that address specific groups and their vulnerabilities. They are too numerous to give in detail here; however, they would include Women's Aid and housing advocacy groups like Shelter.

As you can see from this far from exhaustive list, the needs of people and the range of provision of services to meet need is vast. The examples given in the list represent a few of the many agencies and organisations with whom you may have practice placement opportunities. You will not have sufficient practice placement opportunities to gain a comprehensive understanding of the various contexts in which social work is practised. This is all the more reason why it is important to think about and undertake a little research into the placements you might be interested in. You are unlikely to be able to 'choose' your placement for reasons previously given but you are likely to be asked to identify a type of service provision or service user group you would like work in or with or to express a preference for your placements. So list your placement preferences from an informed position rather than guesswork.

REFLECTION POINT

The first part of this chapter has considered some key issues about practice placements, identified the criteria you will be assessed against whilst on placement and introduced some service user groups and service provision with whom you could obtain practice placements.

This chapter has recommended that you:

- *Read the documents identifying the knowledge, skills and values you will be expected to demonstrate competence in and assessed against while on placement. Familiarise yourself with these. (The current versions are reproduced at the end of this book.)*

- *Prepare for your placement. Complete the documentation required, think about the type of placement you would like to have in terms of the anticipated learning experience and any practical and emotional implications.*

- *Consider what your dress and presentation is saying to your service user. Ensure this is appropriate to your role. Establish and maintain a professional relationship with the people you work with.*

Who's who in practice placements

The following titles used to describe roles and meetings are generic in nature but may not be universally applied. Some of the terms your particular university uses may vary slightly from the ones used here, nevertheless the principles behind the names are sound and applicable.

The placement co-ordinator

This person will be based at the HEI and is responsible for arranging your placement. They, or faculty staff assisting them, will ask for expressions of interest in types of placement and, where possible, arrange placements to match, but this is a negotiated process as previously stated. They or faculty staff assisting them will ensure any necessary pre-placement documentation is completed. The placement co-ordinator will maintain an 'arm's length' oversight of how the placement is progressing but would become involved in the event of any concerns being raised by any of the people involved. A key part in arranging the placement is ensuring the allocation of a practice educator whose role is central to your placement.

The practice educator or PE (also known as practice teacher or assessor)

This person is responsible for assessing your practice during your placement and making a recommendation as to whether you have passed the placement or failed it. Provided that the placement is formally assessed against the NOS and is not an observational or non-assessed placement, they will be a qualified and experienced practitioner who will be likely to hold or be undertaking a qualification or training in practice educating or teaching. They will schedule a series of supervision meetings with you over the duration of the placement, part of which will be dedicated to their assessing the evidence you will offer claiming, through your practice, that you have demonstrated competence in the NOS and VR you identify. The practice educator (PE) will also undertake direct observations of your practice and verify you have undertaken the work you have claimed to have done while on placement. They will write a report that supports their recommendation, describing how you have met the key roles and VR.

The PE is expected to make a commitment to you in undertaking their role and is responsible for overseeing the quality of your learning experience during your placement. Usually the PE and/or the placement receive a specific payment for undertaking this role, which is vital for both you and the profession.

If the PE is based at the placement they may also be your line manager, responsible for allocating your work and accountable for the work you are carrying out on behalf of the agency or organisation you are representing while on placement. If they are not based at the placement, the role of practice educator and line manager may be split, the PE being responsible for assessing practice, the recommendation and PE's report, and an 'on site supervisor' fulfilling the role of line manager.

On site supervisor or OSS (where necessary)

This person is usually your line manager or work-based supervisor and they are responsible for the work allocated to you and carried out on the placement. They will not be responsible for assessing your practice against the NOS, making the pass/fail recommendation or the report, but they will be invited to make a contribution, in their capacity, as to how you have performed as a practitioner. They will also schedule some supervision meetings with you over the duration of the placement, the focus of which will be the work you are undertaking with those service users allocated to you, your recording of that work and any other matters concerned with the agency. This is in contrast to meetings with your practice educator, which will be concerned with considering the evidence you provide to demonstrate competence, and the application of values, theory and legislation.

It will be useful for your on site supervisor (OSS) and your practice educator to meet and for the on site supervisor to comment on your ability as a practitioner as appropriate; for example, they could provide valuable supporting evidence for Key Role 5: *Manage and be accountable, with supervision and support, for your own social work practice within your organisation*.

Support from the university

You are likely to be allocated a contact person from the university whose role is to offer support, should a need arise from the student, PE or OSS. They may also attend, or receive completed documentation from, one or two of the meetings usually undertaken to set up and review the placement and its progress. They are not involved in assessing your practice or managing you or your work while on placement. They would become involved if there were any concerns in respect of the placement.

Important meetings regarding your placement

Based on what you have read so far, you will be in no doubt as to the importance of practice placements and how crucial they are to your progress. In order to give your placement the best chance of being successful it is recommended that the following series of meetings is held.

1. An informal meeting between the student and the proposed PE prior to the placement commencing

Although this tends to be optional, it is regarded as good practice to meet informally with your practice educator, to introduce yourself and chat through the sort of learning experience the PE feels they and the work the placement undertakes can offer you. It is not about you approving or rejecting the offer of the placement, but you do need to feel that you and the PE can work together and you need to feel confident that the placement can meet your learning needs. In the unlikely event that this informal meeting revealed a potential problem in either of these areas, you could speak with your placement co-ordinator about any concerns in advance of your placement starting, which is clearly advantageous.

2. The placement learning agreement meeting

This meeting is usually mandatory and is a formal meeting held in the placement setting within the first weeks of the placement commencing. The people who normally attend are: the student, the practice educator, the on site supervisor (where appropriate) and the university contact person (this may be optional but it is good practice if they attend).

The purpose of the meeting is to formally agree the placement and the roles of the people present. The details of what each will undertake during the placement and the respective expectations of those involved are usually clarified. The way in which the learning opportunities provided by the placement will offer the student scope to demonstrate competence in the NOS and VR should also be discussed, as should the arrangements for and the frequency of supervision. This agreement is usually written up, signed, dated and reviewed further on into the placement. The date for the review should be agreed at this meeting.

3. Review of the learning agreement, or mid-point review

At some time near the mid-point of the placement the learning agreement meeting should be reviewed. The student, practice educator and on site supervisor (where appropriate) should attend. The university contact person may attend. The purpose of this meeting is threefold: (1) to check that what was agreed at the learning agreement meeting is occurring and that those signatories are fulfilling their role in the manner expected; (2) to ascertain that an appropriate level of progress is being made in respect of evidence being gathered and assessed relating to the student achieving competence; and (3) to identify what evidence remains outstanding and how this will be incorporated into the remainder of the placement. An opinion is usually sought from the PE as to whether or not the student is 'on course' for successful completion. This meeting is usually the last one to formally address issues about the placement unless concerns are raised.

Concerns meetings

At any point during the placement the student, practice educator, on site supervisor (where applicable) or the university may request a meeting be convened to discuss any concerns they have about the placement. This could be regarding the quality of learning experience provided, or the progress the student is making. The people that should attend include the student, PE, OSS (where applicable), the university contact person and/or the placement co-ordinator. Unless the concern is a disciplinary matter or a serious concern about the conduct of the student, such as breach of the Codes of Practice, the first of any such meetings is unlikely to result in the suspension or termination of the placement. It is more likely that the concerns are identified and agreement reached as to what needs to be done to address them, by whom and over what timescale.

Supervision meetings

Your supervision meetings are an important aspect of your learning experience during your placement. The frequency and duration of your supervision should be agreed at your learning agreement meeting. It should be undertaken by your practice educator unless you have an on site supervisor, in which case who would undertake what and in what proportion should be agreed at your learning agreement meeting. Basically your PE will be concerned with your progress toward meeting the NOS, VR and how you are linking the more theoretical aspects of social work into your practice. Your OSS will be primarily concerned with the work you are doing on behalf of the organisation they work for. However, supervision in social work, wherever you are in your career, should comprise three elements: *accountability* (what you are doing with your service users on behalf of the organisation), *support* (this could include emotional support for professional or personal issues that are likely to affect your performance or well-being) and *professional development* (this includes considering the knowledge you need to do your job effectively and ensuring you can access this through training courses; for employees this element also considers continuous professional development and appraisal) (Brockbank and McGill, 1998). Not every supervision session will need to address each of the three elements but allowing supervision to become exclusively about accountability will result in your work feeling solely task-orientated and process-driven.

Preparing for your learning agreement meeting and review meeting

As a general principle you should undertake some preparation for any meeting you are going to participate in, especially if you are unaccustomed to your role, and this is true for all the meetings described in this section. Have a few questions in mind for your informal meeting with your proposed PE. Both the learning agreement and placement review meetings are likely to have pro-forma documents and there may be parts of these that require completion in advance of the meeting. Having done so in preparation for the meeting is much more impressive than realising you should have done so when at the meeting! These documents form part of your practice curriculum or portfolio and make an important contribution to the structure of your placement.

Preparing for supervision

CASE STUDY

Picture this scenario. Jim is a student on his first placement and Sarah is his practice educator.

Jim arrives at Sarah's office five minutes late for their supervision. He had rushed back from a visit, and requested a few minutes to go to get his supervision folder. He has no agenda items but included in Sarah's was the request she made last time that Jim brings the reflective logs for the first four weeks of the placement for her to see what issues he is picking up on. Jim apologises and says he has yet to complete them. They go on to discuss some of the work Jim has been doing. Jim enthusiastically describes how he had met service user A, an adult male with learning disabilities, and the work he is doing with him looking at opportunities to assist him to live independently. Sarah asked Jim if he had thought of any theoretical models that might represent service user A's situation and Jim's work in identifying resources for him in the community. Jim looked blank and Sarah suggested that he read something on systems theory for the next time they are due to meet. Jim agreed to do this, and asked Sarah when this was as he had not got his diary with him.

Continued

What are your initial impressions?

Jim appears eager and willing to learn to become a social worker but are you impressed with his organisational and time management skills and the preparation for this supervision session with his practice educator?

A contrasting scenario is one in which the student was on time, with the documents for discussion, proactive in preparing for supervision with an agenda and had thought about some issues for discussion. This student is developing professionalism, something all PEs are looking to see in their students.

The stages of a placement

There are distinct stages in the life of a placement which are often characterised by how you, the student on placement, feel about the placement experience. There are usually three stages: the first is induction and introduction and is characterised by you feeling like a stranger in a place in which everyone else seems familiar. It is appropriate during this initial phase for you to feel somewhat de-skilled and lacking in confidence but this will decrease as you approach the second stage. Stage two begins at the point where the sense of being a stranger is replaced with becoming familiar yourself and developing an understanding of what is provided, to whom and in what way. The transition is complete when you feel you are functioning like a practitioner, albeit a new one, and characterised by a sense of 'Yes, I can do this', suffused with confidence in your ability. The third stage is concerned with winding down and characterised by endings. Most endings have mixed emotional connotations, a sense of loss over some colleagues and service users coupled with the anticipation of moving on to the next year of your course or employment.

The practice portfolio

The practice portfolio is the document you will submit as a testament to the learning achieved while on placement. It will contain the evidence you have relied on to demonstrate competence in the NOS and VR, the PE's recommendation and report, your report and identified future learning needs, to be addressed in a subsequent placement or, if this is a final placement, early career. These essential items are common to all assessed portfolios.

There may be other items which your HEI specify must be present in your portfolio. These may be common items to most assessed portfolios but, as stated in the first part of the chapter, the exact detail of the way your practice curriculum is required to be complied with will depend on the HEI's programme you are attending and the way your course leaders have designed the practice element of the course. Other documents that may be a common requirement in portfolios include: the learning agreement and mid-point review, a student and placement profile, a précis of learning gained on any previous placement, reports on the direct observation of your practice your PE has undertaken, examples of service user feedback on your work with them, and any other means by which your course has required you to provide evidence of competence. For example, you might include reflective journals or logs, summaries of specific work undertaken with service users or an analysis of a piece of work undertaken on placement. Wherever you make reference to a service user you must remove all means by which they may be identified so as to maintain confidentiality. Specific guidance on writing these pieces of work is offered in Chapter 3.

Writing the practice portfolio is a cumulative process across the duration of the placement. Your practice educator should ask to see completed parts of the required curriculum at regular intervals, during supervision. Do not leave substantial parts of this to be written up during the third stage of the placement, as doing so is likely to result in time management problems.

Problems on placement

The majority of placements proceed to a successful conclusion without any difficulties. This is because the selection of students and their Fitness to Practise assessment are rigorous processes and PEs are experienced practitioners and skilled in assessing competence. However, this is an assessed process and PEs have responsibilities to you, the student, but are also accountable for maintaining the quality of practitioners in the profession and to protect service users from people who are unsuitable to become qualified social workers. So, the role of practice educator is important from a number of perspectives but the most significant one for you is the power invested in the PE to make a recommendation to the practice assessment panel as to whether or not you have passed your placement.

There is an indisputable power difference between you and your PE. It is your practice that is coming under scrutiny and so it should be, but you can feel quite vulnerable and dependent upon your PE. Good practice educators are aware of this and will seek ways to ease this dynamic a little. For example, they may suggest you observe their practice before they observe yours. However, the most significant way in which this sense of vulnerability can be nullified is through your PE's feedback on how your practice is developing based on the evidence you are providing. Their recommendation is arrived at cumulatively and you should become increasingly aware of your ability, your strengths and areas for development as your placement proceeds. You should certainly know if you are on course to pass the placement at the mid-point review.

In addition to making a pass/fail placement recommendation practice educators are responsible for overseeing your learning experience on placement. This does not mean they are solely responsible for providing the learning experiences on placement, as a number of people will be contributing to this – colleagues within the placement, colleagues within the agency and, in associated agencies, service users and *you* (see the section on reflective practice).

Many of the problems that occur on placement can be satisfactorily addressed within the placement, provided they are raised in a timely manner and not 'sat on'. A concerns meeting should be convened to air the problem and to decide who needs to do what to resolve it. Occasionally, where insufficient evidence is being provided or it is of insufficient quality, additional time in the placement or a short placement elsewhere may be required. Sometimes the student will be asked to retake the whole placement. This is uncommon but can happen where there are significant shortfalls in the demonstration of competence and attempts to address problems through the concerns meeting have not been successful and the PE's recommendation is a fail. In extreme situations that would lead to disciplinary action if the student were an employee, such as forming inappropriate relationships with service users, misuse of any information gained on placement, gross negligence or serious infringement of the Codes of Practice, the student would fail the placement and may not be offered another, resulting in termination of the course. Your course material will contain specific information on the process and action to be undertaken in the event of a problem on placement.

Consider the following two case studies: sometimes it is not always the service user that needs empowering.

CASE STUDY

Jayne started her level two practice placement at a family centre in an urban area of a large city. She was looking forward to her placement though she was a little apprehensive as this was her first placement and she was not familiar working with the client group. Her PE also worked in the family centre and was very experienced working with families. The learning agreement meeting took place and Jayne settled in.

Initially she undertook some supervised contact, attended a parenting group, and began work on a parenting assessment. She enjoyed the direct work with children, she knew she had ability in communication with children and was relaxed in their company. Working with some of the parents she found much more challenging. There was one whom she found quite intimidating and with whom she was supposed to be undertaking a parenting assessment. This service user had seemed angry and aggressive on their second session and at one point had called into question Jayne's knowledge and experience, saying she was young enough to be her daughter and enquired if she had any kids herself, to which Jayne had said no, to which the mother replied, 'Well what do you know?' Jayne had not known what to say. She felt embarrassed about this encounter and did not tell anyone about it, but it left her feeling undermined and doubting her abilities. She felt sick at the prospect of working with this mother and cancelled the next appointment so as to avoid the situation. It was not as bad with other service users, some of whom she got on well with, but this was a significant piece of work and she did not say anything to her PE as she thought it would look bad and go against her, even though in her heart of hearts she knew her denial was only compounding the problem.

In supervision Jayne's PE enquired how the parenting assessment was going, to which Jayne replied that she was working on the child's developmental needs (this was in part true, as she was comfortable working with the child; it was the parenting capacity section that she was avoiding). Mary, Jayne's PE, asked to see a draft of the parenting assessment at the next session. At the following supervision session Jayne presented the draft assessment which comprised solely an assessment of the child's developmental needs despite Jayne having had the case for three weeks. Mary asked if there was a reason for the lack of progress and Jayne tearfully admitted to what had happened.

Continued

Mary was sympathetic but disappointed that Jayne had not shared this problem with her earlier, after the altercation in fact. Mary said she would have to discuss it at the mid-point review to be held the following week as she was concerned that the problem was not addressed, which brought into question Jayne's professional accountability. At the review it was agreed that Jayne would be supported to complete the parenting assessment, and that Mary would have to feel confident in Jayne's preparedness to share anything that would have a bearing on her work, even if it meant extending her placement, as this was part of being professionally accountable.

COMMENT

What should have happened ...

Following the encounter with the parent, Jayne discussed what had happened and how she was feeling with Mary. Jayne said she had not handled it well but acknowledged her vulnerability to this particular criticism. Mary said that age and having children yourself does not in itself guarantee the acquisition of good childcare practices: if it did there would be fewer service users requiring support! However, knowledge of child development, attachment theory and being skilled in communication with children, all of which Jayne had, promote good childcare practices and Jayne needed to calmly advise the parent of this at their next meeting. Jayne did this and felt much better as a result and continued on schedule with the assessment.

CASE STUDY

Jason had started his placement two months ago with an organisation that offered support to people with sensory impairment. His learning agreement meeting had gone well, with his PE, OSS and he having understood each other's roles and responsibilities. Jason was being allocated work, which he was undertaking, but the arrangements for his supervision were not working out in the manner agreed. The PE and OSS had each agreed to provide 1½ hours per fortnight. Initially this had happened, but then there were a couple of cancellations without alternative appointments being offered. Jason thought they were both very capable and committed to the service users but they were very busy people and they did not seem to have enough time. Even when he did have supervision it started late and was interrupted with phone calls. His PE had apologised and suggested Jason email her material but he really needed one-to-one contact to discuss the application of theory to practice and values. He felt he needed direction on this, but his PE said he seemed to be getting on well. He needed more specific feedback and confirmation that the claims for evidence he was making were appropriate. He had asked his OSS, who seemed to regard his enquiry as a bit of an imposition, replying that this was his PE's role.

Jason felt in a dilemma: on one hand he needed guidance and support, on the other he did not want to moan or imply he could not just 'get on with it', as was appearing

Continued

increasingly to be expected. If Jason did raise it he was worried that it would strain his working relationships; he did not want to become a nuisance or 'make waves' as this could go against him, he thought. Jason persevered with receiving less than half of the time for supervision agreed he would receive. At the mid-point review his PE and OSS said he was on track to pass the placement. He did not raise the inadequacy of his supervision as an issue at the meeting as he thought that doing so might jeopardise his progress.

On completion of the placement the PE recommended a pass. However, Jason's portfolio was referred by markers at the university due to insufficient evidence of competence and links to theory and policy and legislation.

COMMENT

What should have happened ...

Once Jason considered that the inadequacy of his supervision was likely to become a feature of his placement rather than a 'one off' missed appointment he made contact with the support person from the university and discussed the problem. This person reiterated that it was Jason's right to receive supervision in accord with what was agreed because when a placement is offered payment is made, in acknowledgement of the tacit agreement that the PE has the time to undertake the tasks involved. The university contact said that the problem needed to be raised with the PE and asked if Jason would feel comfortable doing this or did he want a meeting to be convened to address it. Jason agreed to speak to his PE about it in the first place and if the situation did not improve he would ask for a meeting to be convened.

Jason did raise it with his PE, who admitted that this had slipped, and the agreed level of supervision was restored.

These two case studies have one thing in common: they both involve confronting a potential conflict. Unless you have an inclination to be confrontational, which is not advised, confronting a problem is something most of us approach with unease and discomfort, so much so that sometimes we opt for the ostrich strategy of 'burying our head in the sand' in the hope that the problem will go away. The difficulty with this is that 'the problem' will not simply 'go away'. Problems have to be addressed if they are to be resolved. Being assertive is an essential skill in interpersonal communication. On any practice placement there is a tension between 'becoming another worker' and having a student's learning experience. Good placements achieve a balance of the two roles. Where one comes to dominate at the expense of the other something needs to be said and adjustments made, otherwise the placement will not afford the student an optimal learning experience and problems could develop, resulting in a poor placement experience.

Submission and marking practice portfolios

The compilation of material presented in the portfolio needs to occur progressively over the duration of the placement. There are two reasons for this. Firstly, the nature of the learning experience and evidence you rely on to demonstrate competence need to be gathered and recorded contemporaneously, which means written either at the time or close to the time the event occurred. You are usually allocated study time within the placement to allow you to do this. Secondly, the gap between ending the placement and the portfolio submission date will be insufficient for you to write a substantial amount from notes but will allow enough time for you and your PE to put the final touches to it and complete your respective reports. It is the responsibility of your PE to make a recommendation as to whether you have passed or failed the placement. The portfolio is then submitted and usually marked by university staff. The PE's focus for their recommendation is your practice, which will have to have met the NOS to pass. The focus for university is the academic quality of the portfolio. Some HEIs give a percentage mark, or a grade. Usually these respective assessments complement each other. Any disagreement or dispute between the PE and university would normally be considered by a Practice Assessment Panel, which acts as a quality assurance process for placements, recommendations and the marking of portfolios. Their decision, as with all marks, is subject to ratification at the university's exam board.

The final task is to complete the quality assurance forms for practice learning which, from September 2010, is a mandatory requirement of the GSCC. The forms represent an evaluative audit of the quality of the learning experience the placement has provided and are independently completed by the student, the PE and the university.

CHAPTER SUMMARY

This chapter has introduced practice placements and discussed some important issues that contribute to the quality of the placement experience and are of concern to students and practitioners alike. Considering such issues as placement choice and the learning opportunities they might present, presentation and professional integrity, the personnel involved, the stage and structure of placements and the portfolio and problems in placement will help prepare you for the placement itself. Preparing for a placement from an informed position will go a long way to reducing the anxiety placements have the capacity to generate.

The next chapter helps you build on the confidence you will have gained through having prepared for a placement and considered some of the issues it will present by developing your skills in writing the portfolio and claiming evidence of competence from different sources of information.

FURTHER READING

Brockbank, A and McGill, I (1998) *Facilitating reflective learning in higher education.* Buckingham: SRHE/Open University Press.

A helpful text for students and educators who are interested in taking further their skills in the ability to learn and the facilitation of learning.

Lomax, R, Jones, K, Leigh, S and Gay, C (2010) *Surviving your social work placement.* Basingstoke: Palgrave Macmillan.

An approachable and practical guide to help you make a success of your first practice placement.

Maclean, S and Harrison, R (2009) *Making the most of your practice learning opportunities.* Rugeley: Kirwin Maclean Associates.

A useful reader, written in a workbook style, which contains a wealth of material to help you navigate your practice placements.

Chapter 3
Writing for your practice placements

Introduction

This chapter will consider the skills required to write a good portfolio of practice. It will build on the similarities with the skills required to write assignments and help you develop those required to write about practice. The chapter will consider claiming evidence of competence from different sources of information commonly used in portfolios of practice. The skills required to write descriptively, analytically and critically will be considered and the appropriate style to use within a practice context will be identified. The chapter concludes with the application of reflection in practice, highlighting the importance of developing this skill as an integral part of one's practice.

In Chapter 2 reference was made to the variability in placement number, duration and the particular competences assessed within a particular placement according to the practice curriculum of the HEI concerned. Reference was also made to the likely changes the social work profession is facing due to: the recommendations of the Social Work Task Force, the change of government in 2010 and the recommendations of Professor Eileen Munro, whom the new coalition government has commissioned to report on certain aspects of current practice in relation to child protection. As a consequence there are likely to be changes made to practice placements and the criteria used to assess competence. The Social Work Reform Board, a body charged with carrying forward and implementing the approved recommendations of the Social Work Task Force, has produced a report entitled *Building a safe and confident future: One year on*. This report, published in 2010, makes important proposals concerning wide-ranging aspects of social work, one of which relates to proposed requirements for social work education. This includes proposals for the standardisation of placement structure, as described in the previous chapter, and a new

'Professional Capabilities Framework for Social Workers in England'. It is proposed that nine specified capabilities will be introduced which are intended to create a framework for a rationalised career structure for social workers.

Despite such change being afoot, this section remains highly relevant due to the enduring nature of the overarching objectives of social work. This is because learning the craft of a skilled occupation like social work will continue to evolve but will also involve students undertaking practice placements and being assessed against criteria that will approximate to those currently applied through the GSCC and the NOS, such as effective interpersonal skills and person-centred ethics and values, as these are core skills, central to a caring profession and the principles for applying them remain the same. I will therefore use examples from the NOS and the Values Requirements when discussing how to claim evidence in this chapter.

The writing skills you will need to write a good portfolio are the same as those needed for assignments, as described in Chapter 1. You need to write to a good standard of English and provide a coherent account of how your practice is developing in accordance with the criteria you are being assessed against. The difference between an assignment and a portfolio of practice is a quantitative difference, in terms of the word count, and qualitative in terms of the references to personal experiences and claiming evidence, through your practice, that you have demonstrated competence in a prescribed standard. Claiming evidence of achieving a competence-based standard through citing practice is a specific skill which, in order to do it well, requires specific attention, which is why a significant part of this chapter is dedicated to it.

Most assignments are usually between 2000 and 4000 words in length, whereas, depending on the duration of the placement, portfolios of practice may be in the order of 8000 to 25,000 words. Although the format of the portfolio is not standardised and will vary according to the course of the particular HEI attended, the manner in which the evidence is collected and presented will be similar: your practice will be directly observed by your practice educator; you are likely to be required to obtain service user feedback on your practice; you will have to provide some form of account of a piece of work or a period of placement experience, such as a reflective diary or log which describes the context and offers some analysis of your practice. These logs or summaries are likely to have pre-scribed sub-headings that you are expected to address: for example, my practice skills; using theory and particular knowledge; application of legislation, policy and procedures; applying social work values and ethics. The subheadings in your HEI's social work practice curriculum or portfolio may vary a little, nevertheless it is vital that you address them explicitly. In addition to this you may be required to write specifically to a key role, its units and elements. Finally, you are likely to be asked to assess the learning experience the placement has afforded you and to identify your future learning needs in anticipation of the next placement or your career as a newly qualified social worker. You can now see why the practice portfolio is such a significant piece of work and why writing one that is not overly descriptive or repetitious is a challenge.

Claiming evidence for having met Occupational Standards

The National Occupational Standards for Social Work comprise six 'key roles' which are each broken down into a number of units; they themselves are further broken down into elements. When claiming competence you must provide specific information about how a particular piece of your practice or behaviour may be considered to be demonstrative of your competence in the particular element of the particular unit of the particular key role or Values Requirement concerned. Each element is assigned 'performance criteria' which are illustrative examples of the type of information you might draw on when claiming evidence for particular elements. A well-written portfolio will make explicit the connection between the standard and the corresponding piece of practice which the student is claiming to meet and reference to it will also be made in the text, as the following example, using Key Role 1, will show. A poorly written portfolio will either make tenuous connections between the standard and practice or leave the reader to make the connection themselves. The six key roles are reproduced in Appendix 1.

> Key Role 1: Prepare for, and work with individuals [or] families, [or] carers, [or] groups and communities to assess their needs and circumstances.

There are three units in Key Role 1. Unit 1 – Prepare for social work contact and involvement – comprises three elements:

> Element 1.1 Review case notes and other relevant material.
>
> Element 1.2 Liaise with others to access additional information that can inform initial contact and involvement.
>
> Element 1.3 Evaluate all information to identify the best form of initial involvement.

The following extract from a student's reflective account provides a good example of how evidence for demonstrating competence for Unit 1 of Key Role 1 was claimed.

I was allocated a referral made by a health visitor in respect of a toddler and his mother who I shall refer to as service user 'A' to protect her identity. The referral stated that the family comprised Mum, a lone parent to a $3^{1}/_{4}$-year-old boy, there were no siblings. The referral requested that consideration should be given to children's services sponsoring a nursery placement for the child under the provision of support to children in need (S17 Children Act 1989). The Health Visitor had recently undertaken a developmental assessment of the toddler and considered he would benefit from the additional stimulation he may receive from a nursery environment.

I checked the children's services computer system to see if the family were known through previous involvement. Two references came up, the first being a parenting assessment of Mum at the time of her child's birth and some previous involvement from the learning disability team which concerned an educational transition from secondary school. Mum was assessed as having a mild learning disability and had some difficulty reading and writing. I looked up the details of the parenting assessment which concluded that Mum had the capacity to meet her baby's needs. [KR 1, Unit 1, Element 1.1]   *Continued*

COMMENT

You can see how the student's claim for having achieved Element 1.1 is valid. The student provides clear evidence for having sought out and read previous case notes which resulted in two specific pieces of information that informed her approach. These were that (a) Mum had a mild learning disability and (b) She had been assessed as having the capacity to meet her child's needs at the time of his birth.

I contacted the Health Visitor who had made the referral and introduced myself as the [student] social worker the referral had been allocated to and informed her that I would be undertaking an initial assessment using the Framework for the Assessment of Children in Need and their Families in respect of her request. I enquired as to the nature of her concerns and she suggested that the toddler was a little behind in his developmental milestones and that the nursery might help address this. She stressed that the level of stimulation he received at home was not a serious cause for concern but that it was limited as Mum had little support with his care.

To further inform my initial contact and involvement I read up on the assessment framework's three domains and twenty dimensions and identified which were most appropriate to my assessment. I also looked up Mary Sheridan's developmental milestones charts for 'at 3 years' for whilst this is the Health Visitor's area of expertise I felt I needed to have an awareness of this myself. I also looked up the specific provision of family support services under s17 Children Act 1989. [Key Role 1, Unit 1, Element 1.2]

COMMENT

You can see how the student's claim for having achieved Element 1.2 is valid. The student provides clear, sound evidence for having sought additional information from the referrer, the Health Visitor. This additional information provided a qualitative insight into what the Health Visitor considered the child to be lacking in terms of stimulation and how this was manifesting in the child: a slight delay in achieving his developmental milestones. The student also discovered that the Health Visitor did not view this as a serious cause for concern and that the mother had little support with her son's care. The student also equipped herself with three additional sources of information that would further enable the efficacy with which to undertake the task: the assessment framework, the developmental milestones charts and the power the LA had to assist through s17 of the 1989 Children Act. This is good quality evidence with strong, explicit connection between the standard and the practice.

The information I had gathered in preparation for making contact with service user 'A' indicated that writing to her to make an appointment may be inappropriate due to her literacy skills. I suggested to the Health Visitor that we undertake a joint visit where she could introduce me and I could then explain my role and what would happen in response to the Health Visitor's referral. Having established an appreciation of the developmental milestones for the toddler's age, identified the relevant domains and dimensions on the assessment framework and clarified the powers in respect of s17, I felt adequately prepared for making initial contact with the service user and beginning to undertake the task. [Key Role 1, Unit 1, Element 1.3]   *Continued*

> **COMMENT**
>
> *You can see how the student's claim for having achieved Element 1.3 is valid. The student provides clear, good evidence for having evaluated and applied all the information she had gathered to identify the best form of initial involvement. This would exclude simply writing due to the mother's disability. A joint visit with the Health Visitor is appropriate and has additional advantages as indicated. The student feels herself to be equipped to approach the mother and to undertake the task having an understanding of the framework which she will be using, the developmental milestones that helped identify the concern and the powers to assist under s17.*

Claiming values requirements

The values and ethics students are required to demonstrate in their practice are listed (a) to (f) within the NOS. The student must:

(a) Develop awareness of your own values, prejudices, ethical dilemmas and conflicts of interest and their implications on your practice.

(b) Show respect for, and the promotion of:

- each person as an individual;

- independence and quality of life for individuals, while protecting them from harm;

- dignity and privacy of individuals, families, carers, groups and communities.

(c) Recognise and facilitate each person's use of language and form of communication of their choice.

(d) Value, recognise and respect the diversity, expertise and experience of individuals, families, carers, groups and communities.

(e) Maintain the trust and confidence of individuals, families, carers, groups and communities by communicating in an open, accurate and understandable way.

(f) Understand and make use of strategies to challenge discrimination, disadvantage and other forms of inequality and injustice.

As with claiming evidence for the elements of units of key roles, claiming evidence for the application of values is best achieved when the practice and the particular value claimed are explicitly and unambiguously linked.

Continuing to use the reflective account of the case above, the student wrote the following:

In preparing for social work contact and involvement with service user 'A', I obtained information stating that 'A' had a mild learning disability and had some difficulty reading and writing. This alerted me to consider that writing to her to make an appointment to visit her may be inappropriate. I also recognised that assuming everyone to have good

Continued

literacy skills is potentially oppressive. Arranging an initial visit with the Health Visitor had a number of advantages as she was known to 'A' and she could introduce me, avoiding any reliance on written communication or calling unannounced. I consider this to be evidence for demonstrating the value (c) which states: 'Recognise and facilitate each person's use of language and form of communication of their choice'. Although I did not have the opportunity to confirm this would have been her preferred choice, as this was an initial contact, I consider it would have been potentially oppressive and contrary to the spirit of value (c) to have assumed a written letter was the most appropriate form of initial communication. [Evidence of Values and Ethics (c)]

COMMENT

You can see how the student's description of practice is used to claim competence in meeting the three elements in Unit 1 of Key Role 1 and Value Requirement (c). You can also see how the claim for the particular element or value is signposted in the text. The provision of good quality, appropriate claims which are signposted back to the relevant role, unit and element or value are fundamental characteristics of a well-written portfolio.

Making appropriate reference to service users

In claiming competence for NOS and VR you will draw on your work with service users and you will need to identify the particular 'case' in question. You are also required to protect the identity of your service users, so you need a system that achieves both potentially contradictory objectives. Some students change the name of the service users, thus creating a pseudonym, or change the initials of the service user (using their real initials is not acceptable because it is possible to identify them). The problem with this method is that when the pseudonym is used for the first time, the reader needs to be told that the service user's name has been changed for they cannot assume it has been. This problem makes the 'name changed' system a rather clumsy method. For example, 'in my work with John (name changed to protect identity)', or 'in my work with M.N. (initials changed to protect identity)'.

The preferred system is to use a key, set out early in the portfolio. You will note in the first example of how to claim evidence the service user was identified as 'A'. Therefore, in drawing on evidence from working with 'A', the reference may be: 'In my work with A ... or, 'in case A ...'. Accordingly, you denote the other service users you worked with on placement in a similar manner, service user B, or case C and so on. It is recommended that you set out a brief description of the case to give the reader some contextual information in the key, as suggested, early in the portfolio. An example continuing to use the same case is given below.

Table of cases worked with on placement which will be referred to when claiming evidence of competence

Case A: This service user was a female single parent with mild learning disabilities; she had one child, a $3\frac{1}{4}$-year-old boy who had been referred by the Health Visitor with a view to children's services sponsoring a nursery school placement to provide additional stimulation to that provided in the home environment.

Continued

> **Table of cases** *continued*
>
> **Case B:** This service user was an 11-year-old boy who had been referred by his secondary school through concerns of unexplained periods of non-attendance and behavioural problems when he did attend. The referral included additional information regarding the family circumstances. His mother had a physical disability and there had been reported incidents of domestic violence perpetrated by the boy's father against the mother.

Descriptive writing and analytical writing

There is a place for solely descriptive accounts in your portfolio of practice: for example, in The Student Profile and The Practice Learning Setting.

- **The Student Profile** This is usually required to be written and placed at the beginning of the portfolio and comprises a pen picture of the student. This should include: where they are in the progression toward their qualification, any previous experience of working with service users, an outline of any previous placements and an outline of the academic modules undertaken and how this has helped prepare the student for the placement. In effect, it is an introduction of the student to the reader but also serves as an introduction of the student to the placement.

- **The Practice Learning Setting** This is usually required in the portfolio and placed after the student's profile. It is the student's account of the placement: the service it provides, to whom and how many, the catchment area, whether it is located within the statutory, private or voluntary sector, the funding, management and staffing structure, etc.

These two documents 'set the scene' and gives the *context* in which the student comes to the placement and vice versa. They are not required to be analytical but should comprise factual statements and therefore it is appropriate that they are solely descriptive. However, when the student begins to describe their placement experience, through a practice log, diary or similar account, description alone is insufficient. Some description is necessary to give the context but as the placement is a learning experience the student also needs to show what *sense* they are making of the experience, not solely describing it. Hence some *analysis* is required.

The following two accounts are taken from the first practice log written by two students, Alex and Clare. Both students are in similar placements – a respite care home for children with learning disabilities. This is a first placement for both students and neither has had previous experience of working with children with learning disabilities.

As explained at the beginning of this chapter, practice logs may also be termed practice diaries, reflective accounts or summaries, or other term, but by whatever name they are an account of the student's experience on placement over a specific period of time. They sometimes have prescribed subheadings that the student is expected to address. Collectively, these accounts represent a chronology of the developmental progress the student has made over the course of their placement. In addition to other forms of evidence collation they also provide opportunities for the student to claim meeting the NOS. In the two accounts that follows Alex and Clare are addressing the subheading 'My practice skills'.

Account One, written by Alex:

My practice skills

I am part way through my induction to Springfields, an 8-bed respite care home for children with learning disabilities. I had a tour round the home undertaken by my practice assessor who is also one of the team leaders. There is an entrance hall which has a number of corridors running from it, one of these leads to the office and I have spent some time there having a look at the policies and procedures, the children's files and other important administrative things like the duty rota. I am scheduled to be 'on duty' Monday to Friday, 9 till 5 initially but will soon be working a shift pattern like most of the other staff which includes evening and weekend work and with the occasional 'sleep in'. On the tour I was shown the lounge, with TV, a music room, a room called the snoozlum which has soft furnishings, bean bags, etc., subdued lighting and piped music and is used by the children to relax in. Another corridor from the hall leads to the children's bedrooms. The children had made them 'theirs' for the duration of their stay with personal belongings, posters, etc. An important part of my induction concerned health and safety issues such as the fire alarm procedure and the children's medication which is administered by the duty team leader.

The day before yesterday I met some of the children as they returned from school. I was not really prepared for this as I have no previous experience of working with children with learning disabilities. One of the children did not reply when I said "Hello, my name is Alex", he just stared and seemed agitated; another member of staff came to my rescue and introduced the child, adding that he does not speak but uses a signing system called Makaton to communicate. I must learn some of this otherwise I will literally be unable to communicate with some of the children. I have since met all the children currently having respite and have come to appreciate the range and variety of communication used by the children. Some are quite articulate, whereas some supplement their use of verbal communication with visual aids which is facilitated by the staff. I have realised just how important the issue of communication is and the diverse methods of communication used by these children and their carers.

Account Two, written by Clare:

My practice skills

This first week has been a steep learning curve for me as I have not worked with children with learning difficulties before. The home provides respite care to children with a range of issues including autism, Asperger's, severe ADHD and other learning disabilities. Although it has eight beds it has 56 children 'on the books' that use the service for varying lengths of time to give their substantive carers a break. I have had an induction to the home which included important health and safety issues such as the fire drill procedure and the children's medication which is administered by the duty team leader. I have spent time familiarising myself with the home's policies and procedures and have had access to the children's files.

In respect of my practice skills, the biggest issue for me so far has been appreciating the diverse methods of communication used by the children and staff. Apart from specific

Continued

Account Two, written by Clare *continued*

languages such as Makaton and BSL which some children and staff use, the staff showed me some visual aids which are used to supplement verbal language. I had an opportunity to use these with child 'B' who I met yesterday when he came to stay for a week. I remembered from his file that 'B' is on the autistic spectrum and can become agitated if bombarded with verbal information. He asked who was on duty on Saturday and how long he was going to stay. I supplemented my verbal answers that I was not sure he fully understood, with a set of photographs of the staff, pointing out those rostered in to work at the weekend. I also used a calendar to identify the days he was staying here and when he would return home. He seemed content with this information and I thought how I might further use visual aids, for example, the use of pictures in a cookery book to learn about what he likes to eat. I have so much to learn about the children who stay here, they and their needs are so varied but I feel I am beginning to develop my practice skills already and compliance with values requirement (c) (see p 46) through the use of visual aids to assist communication. [Values and Ethics Requirement (c)]

COMMENT

What is your assessment of the two accounts?

Alex's account is largely descriptive and lacks focus despite having used more words than Clare. There are no developing practice skills identified despite the subheading.

Clare's account is more focused. It contains some analysis of what she is seeing. Explicit reference is made to 'My practice skills' and an example given of how her communication skills are developing. She uses the opportunity to refer to demonstrating compliance with a Values Requirement.

There is a lot going on for the student in a 'new' placement with a 'new' group of service users especially where the student is unaccustomed to the particular needs of the service users. The desire to describe the experience in detail can be strong but needs to be resisted. The student's placement experience is of course important and unique to them but the seasoned practitioner, in the role of practice educator, will be looking to see the student beginning to make sense of what they are experiencing through some analysis. This includes the recognition of where learning has taken place and how it was and can continue to be applied.

Direct observations

Direct observations of practice are an important aspect of an assessed placement. Some students feel somewhat daunted by the prospect of being observed and assessed while working but this level of scrutiny is appropriate given the trust invested in the social work role and the vulnerability of many service users. Some programmes require several observations and specify a certain number to be undertaken by the practice educator and with service users. The programme I am most familiar with requires four direct observations to take place: a minimum of two must be undertaken by the practice educator and two must be with service users, as opposed to, for example, the on-site supervisor observing a student's presentation to a team meeting. As with most events, the key for a good outcome lies in preparation.

Sally thought she had prepared for her first direct observation. She was in the seventh week of her first practice placement in a care for the elderly team. She thought that for her first direct observation she would choose something fairly routine, a review of a care package, as she did not want anything too taxing as she knew she would be nervous.

Burt is 79 years old and lives alone. He receives care services at home three days per week. He has help in the home and some personal care; he also receives meals three times per week. This support enabled Burt, a widower who has a serious respiratory condition, to remain at home. Burt's sister, Dora, who lives near Burt, visits most days and provides him with some meals. Sally arranged the review with Dora over the phone and asked if her supervisor could observe her at the meeting, to which Dora agreed. Sally understood from the paperwork that the review should be straightforward as she was unaware of the need for any changes in the care package. The home care provider was going to be present, as were Burt, Dora, Sally and her on-site supervisor, David. However, on the day the observation proved to be a bit of a disaster. Sally did not know Burt was hard of hearing and she found herself having almost to shout for Burt to hear her. He did not appear to understand that the meeting was going to be attended by David, whom Burt did not know, or what his role was. Furthermore, he became quite distressed when Dora enquired if Burt could have some respite care in a home to give her a break. Neither Sally nor Burt had expected this question to arise.

In the verbal feedback following the meeting Sally did not need David to tell her that her preparation for the meeting had been inadequate. While Sally knew of Burt's need for a respirator and the care he must take not to exert himself she missed the fact that he used a hearing aid and had not known that he was currently out of batteries. Sally assumed that Dora would have passed onto Burt her request to have her practice at the meeting observed but Dora had agreed to this without reference to her brother. Sally had also assumed that no one wanted any changes to the care package as she was unaware of any request to do so. However, she had not checked this out in advance of the meeting. Had she done so she could have explored the opportunities for Dora to have a break and the idea of respite much more sensitively. Of course, not every issue that can occur in practice can be anticipated but any concerning communication and proposals for changes in a care package, necessitating a revision of the assessment of need, are fundamental and should be part of a practitioner's engagement and preparation as opposed to being 'discovered' at a formal meeting.

Preparing for a direct observation: things to do in advance

- If you have received feedback from a previous observation(s) think how you might incorporate any points for improvement.

- Decide which elements of which unit and key role you want to demonstrate competence in.

- Select an observable scenario that presents an appropriate opportunity to meet your objectives.

- Obtain the permission of the other person or people involved.

- Explain to them that it is your practice that is being observed and that any notes taken by the practice educator (PE) will be restricted to this.

- Arrange a mutually convenient time and venue for the observation to take place.

- Consider the need for any transport arrangements/directions for your PE.

- Rehearse what you anticipate happening. Reduce the risk of any 'surprises' by checking out if there are any significant 'new' issues people want to raise in advance. Consider what you might do if something unexpected occurred.

Things to do on the day of the observation

- Ensure your PE knows the context in which the observation is occurring if you have not already done so.

- Ensure you have any leaflets or information you need with you.

- Allow yourself sufficient time to get to the venue and be on time.

- On arrival check with the service user that it remains alright for the observation to go ahead as discussed and restate the confidentiality issues. Introduce your observer.

- Think about the room and seating arrangements (proxemics). You and the service user need to be placed in relation to one another to best undertake the task (interview/counselling, etc). The observer needs to be able to see but be unobtrusively positioned.

- If another appointment with the service user is required, ensure you have your diary with you so you can make it there and then.

- At the conclusion of the observation, thank the service user.

After the observation

- Understand how you are going to receive feedback: a brief verbal summary may be given initially, followed up in writing.

- Appraise your performance yourself; does it correspond with that of your observer?

Obtaining service user feedback

Most portfolios of assessed practice will require evidence from one or more service users giving a snapshot, from their perspective, of what it was like to work with you. Some consideration of which service user to ask to provide this and the manner in which the information is gathered and presented needs to be undertaken for the exercise to be meaningful and not perfunctory. Some practice curricula will have pro-forma documentation for this but these often curtail creativity and tend not to be 'tailor made' to the service user group or individual you have selected. Where you can create your own format for feedback consideration needs to be given to the method you propose to use. A short questionnaire is commonly used, but again thought needs to go into the questions and the way the 'answers' are expected to be presented. Are they appropriate for the cognitive ability of your service user(s)? Do they address what your PE wants to know? Can the process be made interesting, entertaining even, or is it bound to be similar to the ubiquitous 'evaluation' exercise so often experienced? Are your 'questions' designed to elicit 'yes' or 'no' responses or are you going to invite some narrative comment?

The sort of information you and your practice assessor should be interested in relates to your interpersonal communication skills and professional competence and may include: Was X friendly and approachable? Did you feel you were listened to by X? Did X explain their role? Was X knowledgeable? The way these questions are phrased will elicit a 'yes' or 'no' response, which may be desired, but a more qualitative response could be obtained by grading the response: On a scale of 1 (low) to 10 (high) did X do what they said they were going to? Or you could elicit a narrative response by asking: What was it you liked about working with X?

A student of mine who was working with three children aged between five and eight in a pre-adoptive placement designed her feedback around the Humpty Dumpty nursery rhyme. It took the form of an activity that involved drawing, cutting out face shapes and expressions and attaching them to a flip-chart-size 'wall' they had made with Humpty sitting on the top. Her second example of feedback was drawn from members of a placement preparation group to whom she had presented a session on life story book work. Her feedback took the form of a short questionnaire in which the questions were centred on her aims and objectives in the presentation. These examples demonstrate how the feedback may be gathered from very different service users, the first being a fun activity, the second being more focused and formal. In addition to considering who to ask for feedback, the timing of when feedback is sought is also important and needs to be obtained upon or after completion of the work undertaken with the service user(s). Seeking feedback from groups has the advantage of allowing responses to be anonymous but, in any event, in your portfolio you must protect the identity of any service user from whom you have obtained feedback.

Writing from a critical perspective

Writing critically requires you to write from a critical perspective. It is concerned with representing what you are writing about, a policy, procedure, legislation, theory or practice, with sufficient confidence to appraise it. Any appraisal comes to some conclusions about what was included or achieved, what was ignored or not attempted and what was not included or achieved: it is a *qualitative* assessment. To write from a critical perspective successfully requires a balanced, well-informed understanding of the topic.

At the beginning of this chapter an example was given about how to claim an element of a unit of a key role of one of the NOS, and a student's account was used as an illustration. The student referred to an assessment they were to undertake to inform a decision about the sponsorship of a child's nursery school placement under s17 of the Children Act 1989. The assessment tool used was the Framework for the Assessment of Children in Need and their Families 2000. We are going to refer to this framework to consider a descriptive, analytical and critical account. The context in which these accounts occur is a part of a student's reflective log, in which they are writing to the subheading: Using theory and particular knowledge.

Account One

Using theory and particular knowledge

I used the Framework for the Assessment of Children in Need and their Families (2000) to help inform my knowledge of the circumstances and decision making process in respect of my work with case 'A'. The framework cites the child and the aim of safe-guarding and promoting their welfare at the centre of a triangle, the sides of which identify three domains: Child's Developmental Needs, Parenting Capacity, and Family and Environmental Factors of the child's world. Within each of these, a total of 20 relevant dimensions are listed (see diagram 1).

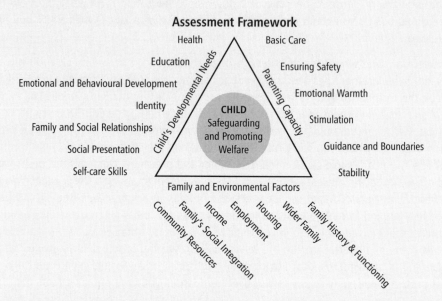

Assessment Framework

I used this framework to undertake an initial assessment of the 3-year-old child's needs in relation to the specific dimensions of stimulation from the Parenting Capacity domain, education and health and behavioural development from the Child's Developmental Needs domain and wider family, income and community resources from the Family and Environmental Factors domain. I selected these particular dimensions on the basis that they were the most relevant and 'at issue' to address the Health Visitor's request that Children's Services sponsor a nursery place for 'A's son in order to provide additional stimulation to that which he was being provided with within the home. Through the assessment, a need for this provision was substantiated and the outcome was that a place was funded for two mornings per week. [Evidence for KR1, Unit 3, Element 3.3 see p 63]

COMMENT

As a result of what you already understand about descriptive writing you should now be able to see that the above account is solely that. Accordingly, it is a poor account that fails to tell the reader what the worker really did with the information provided by the service user. Repeating the dimensions themselves does not tell you what sense the worker made of them. What the account really needs is some analysis.

Account Two

Using theory and particular knowledge

I used the Framework for the Assessment of Children in Need and their Families (2000) to help inform my knowledge of the circumstances and decision making process in respect of my work with case 'A'. The framework is ecological and representative of the child's whole world as it has the child and the aim of safeguarding and promoting their welfare at the centre of a triangle, the sides of which identify three key domains across which specific dimensions are identified.

The most relevant domains and dimensions were identified and used to undertake an initial assessment of the 3-year-old child's needs in relation to the referral. These were: stimulation *from the Parenting Capacity domain. I gathered information about the other children and people the child regularly came into contact with, the amount of time Mum had to give him for interactive play and the type of toys and other age-appropriate items the child had access to. An assessment of the information and analysis as to whether or not the amount of stimulation the child was exposed to was sufficient to afford him the opportunity to achieve or maintain a reasonable standard of health or development was made, the outcome of which was that the child would benefit from the provision of additional stimulation to that currently offered.*

This concurred with the Health Visitor's developmental assessment of the child which suggested he was beginning to fall behind in the dimensions of: education *and* health and behavioural development, *from the Child's Developmental Needs domain. She did not consider there were any congenital concerns that needed referring on and so it was reasonable to conclude that exposure to additional stimulation would address the issue. I also considered the dimensions of* wider family, income *and* community resources *from the Family and Environmental Factors domain. I selected these dimensions to explore: who may be in a position to provide additional stimulation within the extended family, if Mum had sufficient financial resources to fund a nursery placement, what other resources could be utilised such as a portage service, a toy library or a mums and toddlers group. The resulting options were discussed with Mum and a preferred option agreed which was for Children's Services to sponsor a nursery place subject to periodic review. This decision needed managerial approval but this was given as the assessment confirmed provision under s17 Children Act 1989 was appropriate. [Evidence for KR1, Unit 3, Elements 3.1, 3.2 and 3.3 see p 63]*

COMMENT

As you can see, this is a much fuller account through which you get some insight into the worker's basis for their decision making. This is because the account contains some analysis of the information gathered through the assessment. Although this account uses more words, (a little over 100 more), you will note that a claim for additional evidence is legitimately made for the whole of Unit 3.

Account Three

Using theory and particular knowledge

I used the Framework for the Assessment of Children in Need and their Families (2000) to help inform my knowledge of the circumstances and decision making process in respect of my work with case 'A'. The framework is ecological and representative of the child's whole world as it has the child and the aim of safeguarding and promoting their welfare at the centre of a triangle, the sides of which identify three key domains across which specific dimensions are identified. The framework was introduced to reduce the number, unify and bring some standardisation to assessments on children and their families undertaken by a variety of agencies, hence it is also known as the Common Assessment Framework.

The domains and their dimensions are helpful in offering generic subheadings which, as you proceed with the assessment, you make specific and personal to the child and family concerned. However, a decision needs to be made as to which dimensions are addressed unless a core assessment is required. For example, undertaking an assessment of the basic care dimension would be appropriate where neglect was a concern. So, the exercise of professional judgement is relevant from the start of the assessment process.

The most relevant domains and dimensions identified and used to undertake an initial assessment of the 3-year-old child's needs in relation to the referral were: stimulation from the Parenting Capacity domain. I gathered information about the other children and people the child regularly came into contact with, the amount of time Mum had to give him for interactive play and the type of toys and other age-appropriate items the child had access to. An assessment of the information and analysis as to whether or not the amount of stimulation the child was exposed to was sufficient to afford him the opportunity to achieve or maintain a reasonable standard of health or development was made, the outcome of which was that the child would benefit from the provision of additional stimulation to that currently offered. This decision again called on professional judgement, which relied on knowledge of child development but other less tangible issues such as cultural expectations, attitudes and values both personal and profes-sional are also present, hence the values requirement within the competence framework. There tends to be less emphasis placed on this aspect of 'an assessment' as the role of 'professional judgement' is a problematic concept. However, the analysis of the child's needs concurred with the Health Visitor's developmental assessment of the child which suggested he was beginning to fall behind in the dimensions of education and health and behavioural development, from the Child's Developmental Needs domain. She did not consider there were any congenital concerns that needed referring on and so it was reasonable to conclude that exposure to additional stimulation would address the issue.

The specific issue of risk is not identified in the framework's domains or dimensions but can be a significant factor in many assessments. Although they may be considered 'low key' in respect of this referral, a failure to address the shortfall in stimulation now could have significant consequences for the child's future. I also considered the dimensions of wider family, income and community resources from the Family and Environmental Factors domain. I selected these dimensions to explore: who may be in a position to

Continued

Account Three *continued*

provide additional stimulation within the extended family, if Mum had sufficient financial resources to fund a nursery placement, what other resources could be utilised such as a portage service, a toy library or a mums and toddlers group. Mum did not appear to have much support from extended family and was keen for her son to have the opportunity to play with other children. Mum's main source of income was derived from welfare benefits and she said she could not afford nursery school. She said she would join the toy library and other options were discussed; however, the preferred option was for Children's Services to sponsor a nursery place subject to periodic review. This decision needed managerial approval but this was given as the assessment confirmed provision under s17 Children Act 1989 was appropriate. [Evidence for KR1, Unit 3, Elements 3.1, 3.2 and 3.3 see p 63]

COMMENT

This is a detailed account but contains some insights into applying the framework, part of which includes some critical analysis. This degree of insight is demonstrative of the student's ability not only to undertake an assessment in response to the referral but to also consider the tools used to undertake it. This level of analysis is not limited to the task but includes some commentary on the process.

Citing the use of theories and their frameworks in portfolios of practice

The role of theory within social science is tentative. You will not find the equivalent of Newton's Laws of Motion within social science because unlike objects and their motion people do not react in the *same* way to a given set of circumstances. Most may act in a *similar* way hence a theory may be developed, suggestive of causality, of a possible explanation. There will, however, be some people that do not act in a similar way, some that confound prediction, some that buck the trend. For example, some children who were subjected to an abusive childhood go on to become abusive adults and we may explain this through forms of behaviourism and social learning theory. The problem we have in applying theoretical explanation is that of those children who were subjected to an abusive childhood almost as many do not go on to become abusive adults. On the contrary, many go on to become loving and caring partners and parents.

So, what are we to make of this? Can a theoretical framework help explain this? It is surely inadequate to simply conclude that abusive experiences are very damaging to some and others are unaffected. Where would an initiative like Every Child Matters and its laudable outcomes be if this were the case? Can we assume that all those apparently unaffected or minimally so have all had access to talking therapies? No, but they may have had experiences and other relationships that were not abusive but have had a therapeutic effect. They may have been resilient and tenacious. They may have personal qualities through which others, such as teachers, have conveyed a sense of self-worth and respect. There may have been another 101 things that have been influential in shaping them as their life journey progressed and it can be regarded as presumptuous and potentially oppressive to make assumptions as to causality and explanation of another's behaviour.

So, is there any merit in the attempt to systematically study human behaviour, to develop theories and to apply informed knowledge to social phenomena? Yes, very much so. On what basis would social work intervention be undertaken without the constructs that the application of theory provide? The point is that it will be limited in the extent to which a completely satisfactory 'fit' between a theory and the social phenomena it attempts to explain can be achieved. There will be theories that offer a more substantial explanation of phenomena than others – attachment theory may be a case in point – but even those make a *contribution* to our understanding as opposed to satisfying it. This needs to be remembered by students when they are claiming to have applied theory in their practice. It is perfectly legitimate to offer a qualitative analysis as to the extent to which you considered a theory offered an explanation of a practice situation or an associated method of intervention to be effective: this is after all writing from a critical perspective.

The legitimate use of claims for the application of theories and their frameworks

The extent to which theory explains phenomena is limited, but that does not mean it cannot make a substantial contribution to our understanding and assist us in our thinking about how things might work and make sense. Theoretical frameworks provide us with models upon which we can hang ideas and events and see how they fit, where there is a good fit and where the gaps are, where it is so general it is almost stating the obvious and where it is so specific it is difficult to apply. The other main use of theory is that it gives rise to associated methods of intervention. For example, behaviour modification through rewards or punishments is an intervention whose theoretical origin is a form of behaviourism known as operant conditioning. Family therapy is an intervention whose theoretical origin is systems theory, as are holistic and ecological approaches.

The most common error students make when citing the application of theory in their practice portfolio is either to simply state the name of the theory they claim to have used, for example 'I used brief solution therapy in my work with service user X' without actually telling the reader what they did and why what they did was an application of brief solution therapy. The other common mistake is for the student to list a number of theories as bullet points adding that they had used them, again the error being failing to tell the reader what they did and why what they did was an application of the theory. In both cases the student fails to expose their knowledge of the theory and its application.

It is important that students only lay claim to use a theory that they actually understand and apply its associated method of intervention to an appropriate extent. 'Appropriate' here is intended to mean realistic in the context of practice and with regard to the service user's involvement and participation. For example, it may be entirely appropriate to take a personal history from your service user although this intervention has its roots in psychodynamic theory. However, it would not be appropriate for the social worker to engage the service user in psychotherapy unless they were trained as a psychotherapist and this form of intervention was agreed to and distinct from the particular aims of the social work intervention. So, when claiming the application of theory to practice, identify the theoretical construct that has informed your approach and be specific about how you applied its associated method of intervention.

Reflective writing and becoming a reflective practitioner

A lot of emphasis is placed on reflection in social work practice. You will be expected to demonstrate your ability to reflect and show you are capable of becoming a reflective practitioner in your work on placement and provide evidence of this in your portfolio. As with most things, it is a concept that is amenable to layers of complexity. Here, I want to introduce it in its most simple form. Reflective practice, in essence, is the conscious and deliberate commitment to learn from experience. Before we continue we must consider if it is possible to learn from experience and if it is, what environment is best suited for doing so.

Do we learn from experience? How many times, when we have woken with a thick head, throbbing with the result of the previous night's excesses, have we said 'never again'? And yet, we have done it again. While we would claim to be rational beings this is hardly representative of rational behaviour. The fact that our idea of having a good time can result in our feeling ill is a curious association, if not strange! You may have been working with a woman on placement, helping her to empower herself to rid herself of an abusive partner only to later discover that her new partner is also abusive. So what is the answer to the question 'Do we learn from experience'? Based on these examples the answer is no! However, if we ask ourselves if we *can* learn from experience the answer has to be yes, as each experience presents us with an opportunity to learn from it, even if that learning is limited to deciding whether we would want to repeat that experience or not.

We have established that we do not always learn from experience but that we can do and many of us, of course, do. This leads us to ask what must be present for us to learn from experience.

- A willingness to do so must be present, so we are back to motivation again – can we be bothered?

- An ability to do so must be present, which is about cognition – an ability to 'think it through' must be present.

- An experience that is amenable to being learnt from must also be present, though perhaps more are than are learnt from.

- Then there are 'climactic issues', such as having sufficient time, energy and an absence of high stress levels to enable sufficient space to metaphorically 'stand back' from the practice experience to view it from other perspectives and undertake some analysis of it.

Now consider this comment you hear a student make on leaving a lecture: 'That lecture was useless, not worth getting out of bed for.' This statement may well be true for the student concerned and it can be left there, perhaps only serving a purpose when the student is setting their alarm clock the following week. Another student who attended the lecture had a similar opinion but went on to comment: 'The lecturer mumbled, looked down at notes nearly all the time and did not make eye contact with the audience.' This student has analysed *why* the lecture was poor: it was due to ineffective engagement and communication between the lecturer and the audience. A third student was of a similar opinion to the first, analysed the reasons why, like the second, but went on to say, 'When I deliver my presentation next term I will ensure I project my voice and make eye contact with my audience'. This student used the experience to learn from and identified the skills they would need to use and may need to practise for their forthcoming presentation. The third student used the experience and applied their learning to a future event. This student has begun to demonstrate the skills of reflection. Applying reflection to practice situations is a prerequisite of becoming a reflective practitioner.

Including examples of reflective writing in your portfolio will demonstrate to the reader that you recognise experiences are often learning opportunities and that you are actually learning from practice experiences and applying that learning. Such learning is not limited to what you did or what you saw someone else do but, in the light of what happened, what you *could* have done or what someone else *could* have done differently. The playing out of alternative scenarios and the ability to consider their likely respective outcomes, in accord with different actions and interventions, is a complementary skill to critical analysis and appraisal previously discussed.

We can see an example of reflective practice in another excerpt from the student's reflective log discussing the work undertaken with service user 'A' but this time the student is addressing the subheading: Applying social work values and ethics.

Applying social work values and ethics

In my work with service user 'A' one of the dimensions I assessed was stimulation, particularly that provided by or through the child's mother, as this was in the parenting capacity domain and highly relevant to the matter at hand. I was aware that she had received services for a mild learning disability in her youth and although she was not in receipt of any services regarding this since becoming an adult, I had to consider if this had a bearing on the provision of stimulation for her son. On reflection this presented a dilemma for me (value 'a') as I would have been remiss in not considering this yet I did not want to contribute to any oppression or discrimination she may suffer as a result of disability. I was mindful of the fact that I might well have been responding to a referral where the circumstances were similar but where Mum did not have a learning disability, consequently I avoided assuming that the mother's learning disability was a causal factor in her son's needs for additional stimulation. To have assumed it was would clearly have been discriminatory (value 'f'). I raised this in supervision with my practice educator and we had a discussion which I found helpful in working out an approach that satisfied social work values and ethical practice. We concluded that such a factor does need to be considered in an assessment in order to gain an idea of Mum's understanding of her son's need of stimulation, and the quality of what was provided was fundamental to the assessment. However, any shortfall could be the result of a variety of factors as well as any cognitive limitation. These may include a lack of knowledge of an appropriate level of stimulation, or the lack of age-appropriate toys, or too much TV, or insufficient interactive play with others. These contributory factors to a shortfall in a level of stimulation could be addressed

Continued

Applying social work values and ethics continued

through giving information and this is what happened with 'A'. She was keen to do her best for him and through our work together she engaged him in more interactive play, and joined a toy library to increase his choice of age-appropriate toys. We arranged for him to attend nursery two mornings a week so he would have the opportunity to play with other children. [Evidence claimed for Values and Ethics (a) and (f) see p 46]

CHAPTER SUMMARY

This chapter has considered the skills required to write a good portfolio of practice. The chapter has identified the different sources of information commonly used in portfolios of practice from which evidence of competence is drawn. Consideration was given to how to claim evidence of meeting the occupational standards and values and the need to explicitly connect the practice with the standard or value being claimed was highlighted. The importance of preparing for direct observations of practice was emphasised and the process for undertaking these was considered. Guidance on how best to make reference to work undertaken with service users was offered and examples for obtaining their feedback were given. The skills required to write descriptively, analytically and critically were explored and the appropriate style to use within practice contexts identified. The chapter concluded with demonstrating the application of reflection in practice, highlighting the importance of developing this skill as an integral part of one's professional practice.

In Appendix 1 the National Occupational Standards are reproduced. These standards are the criteria student social workers are currently assessed against, and although some change to these is envisaged, the principles conveyed in this chapter hold good for assessment against any professional standard.

FURTHER READING

Department of Health, Department for Education and Employment, and the Home Office (2000) *Framework for the assessment of children in need and their families.* London: The Stationery Office. Available at **www.dh.gov.uk/**.

This is the standardised assessment tool used to identify the needs of children and young people. It is used by children's services workers to identify children's additional needs and by social care workers when undertaking initial assessments for children in need and core assessments for children with complex needs

General Social Care Council (2002) *Codes of practice for social workers and employers.* London: GSCC.

Student and qualified social workers have to comply with these codes in order to practice ethically and retain their regisration. The codes for social care workers are reproduced in Appendix 3.

Quality Assurance Agency for Higher Education (2008) *Benchmark statements for social work.* **www.qaa.ac.uk** (accessed 28 March 2011).

These statements form the basis for the universities' course content for the degree qualification in social work.

Social Work Reform Board (2010) *Building a safe and confident future: One year on – Detailed proposals from the Social Work Reform Board.* London: Department for Education. Available at **www.education.gov.uk/publications/**.

This document is of fundamental importance to all social care workers as it is the blueprint for the next phase of development of the profession.

Topss UK Partnership (2002) *National Occupational Standards For Social Work.* **www.skillsforcare. org.uk** (accessed 28 March 2011).

These are the standards against which your practice will be assessed whilst on practice placements.

Conclusion

Chapter 1 of this book offered you advice and guidance in respect of the skills you need to achieve a good standard of written English while undertaking a programme of qualification in social work. However, they will not be restricted to your studies; once acquired, these skills will become integrated with your other abilities and serve to improve the quality of your written communication thereafter. Social work practice is as dynamic as the social phenomena it seeks to engage with. Practitioners are subject to change in many aspects of their occupation and with the advent of the Social Work Task Force and resulting Reform Board the next few years will prove no exception. As social work seeks further recognition of professional status following the requirements of a degree qualification and registration, a workforce capable of an exacting standard of written communication is essential.

Chapter 2 offered some basic but essential information regarding issues concerning practice placements and guidance on how best to prepare for and navigate a successful pathway through them. Chapter 3 addressed the application of writing skills for practice placements as manifested through portfolios. The particular skill of demonstrating competence in a practice context by claiming to have met prescribed occupational standards is required and the chapter provides examples of how to achieve this.

In this book, which I hope you have found to be very approachable and readable, I have tried to leave you with an indelible message: that writing well matters. Its importance is not confined to your assignments or your portfolios of practice or indeed your post-qualifying practice. It is one of the principal forms of self expression, a method of communication. Like other forms of communication, it has layers of complexity. It conveys meaning that is not solely limited to the words of which it is constituted. The precision and the art with which the words chosen are used convey a meaning of their own. This not only leaves the reader with an impression of the writer but has a bearing on the outcome that can be contrary to that which was intended. For example: a referral containing incorrect information will lead to an inappropriate response, a written agreement that is ambiguous will lead to confusion, an assessment that is inaccurate will lead to misunderstanding. The clarity with which you write will not merely determine the accuracy of meaning you wish to convey but will be the hallmark of your professionalism. So you can see, time spent on acquiring, improving and honing the skills you need to write well will pay dividends far beyond passing assignments and portfolios of practice. It is an investment in your career!

Appendix 1
National Occupational Standards

Key Role 1: Prepare for, and work with individuals, families, carers, groups and communities to assess their needs and circumstances

Unit 1 – Prepare for social work contact and involvement

1.1 Review case notes and other relevant material.

1.2 Liaise with others to access additional information that can inform initial contact and involvement.

1.3 Evaluate all information to identify the best form of initial involvement.

Unit 2 – Work with individuals, families, carers, groups and communities to help them make informed decisions

2.1 Inform individuals, families, carers, groups and communities about your own, and the organisation's duties and responsibilities.

2.2 Work with individuals, families, carers, groups and communities to identify, gather, analyse and understand information.

2.3 Work with individuals, families, carers, groups and communities to enable them to analyse, identify, clarify and express their strengths, expectations and limitations.

2.4 Work with individuals, families, carers, groups and communities to enable them to assess and make informed decisions about their needs, circumstances, risks, preferred options and resources.

Unit 3 – Assess needs and options to recommend a course of action

3.1 Assess and review the preferred options of individuals, families, carers, groups and communities.

3.2 Assess needs, risks and options taking into account legal and other requirements.

3.3 Assess and recommend an appropriate course of action for individuals, families, carers, groups and communities.

Key Role 2: Plan, carry out, review and evaluate social work practice, with individuals, families, carers, groups, communities and other professionals

Unit 4 – Respond to crisis situations

4.1 Assess the urgency of requests for action.

4.2 Identify the need for legal and procedural intervention.

4.3 Plan and implement action to meet the immediate needs and circumstances.

4.4 Review the outcomes with individuals, families, carers, groups, communities, organisations, professionals and others.

Unit 5 – Interact with individuals, families, carers, groups and communities to achieve change and development and to improve life opportunities

5.1 Develop and maintain relationships with individuals, families, carers, groups, communities and others.

5.2 Work with individuals, families, carers, groups, communities and others to avoid crisis situations and address problems and conflict.

5.3 Apply and justify social work methods and models used to achieve change and development, and improve life opportunities.

5.4 Regularly monitor, review and evaluate changes in needs and circumstances.

5.5 Reduce contact and withdraw from relationships appropriately.

Unit 6 – Prepare, produce, implement and evaluate plans with individuals, families, carers, groups, communities and professional colleagues

6.1 Negotiate the provision to be included in the plans.

6.2 Identify content and actions and draft plans.

6.3 Carry out your own responsibilities and monitor, co-ordinate and support the actions of others involved in implementing the plans.

6.4 Review the effectiveness of the plans with the people involved.

6.5 Renegotiate and revise plans to meet changing needs and circumstances.

Unit 7 – Support the development of networks to meet assessed need and planned outcomes

7.1 Examine with individuals, families, carers, groups, communities and others support networks which can be accessed and developed.

7.2 Work with individuals, families, carers, groups, communities and others to initiate and sustain support networks.

7.3 Contribute to the development and evaluation of support networks.

Unit 8 – Work with groups to promote individual growth, development and independence

8.1 Identify opportunities to form and support groups.

8.2 Use group programmes, processes and dynamics to promote individual growth, development and independence, and to foster interpersonal skills.

8.3 Help groups to achieve planned outcomes for their members and to evaluate the appropriateness of their work.

8.4 Disengage from groups appropriately.

Unit 9 – Address behaviour which presents a risk to individuals, families, carers, groups and communities

9.1 Take immediate action to deal with the behaviour that presents a risk.

9.2 Work with individuals, families, carers, groups, communities and others to identify and evaluate situations and circumstances that may trigger the behaviour.

9.3 Work with individuals, families, carers, groups and communities on strategies and support that could positively change the behaviour.

Key Role 3: Support individuals to represent their needs, views and circumstances

Unit 10 – Advocate with, and on behalf of, individuals, families, carers, groups and communities

10.1 Assess whether you should act as the advocate for the individual, family, carer, group or community.

10.2 Assist individuals, families, carers, groups and communities to access independent advocacy.

10.3 Advocate for, and with, individuals, families, carers, groups and communities.

Unit 11 – Prepare for, and participate in decision making forums

11.1 Prepare reports and documents for decision making forums.

11.2 Work with individuals, families, carers, groups and communities to select the best form of representation for decision making forums.

11.3 Present evidence to, and help individuals, families, carers, groups and communities to understand the procedures of and the outcomes from, decision making forums.

11.4 Enable individuals, families, carers, groups and communities to be involved in decision making forums.

Key Role 4: Manage risk to individuals, families, carers, groups, communities, self and colleagues

Unit 12 – Assess and manage risks to individuals, families, carers, groups and communities

12.1 Identify and assess the nature of the risk.

12.2 Balance the rights and responsibilities of individuals, families, carers, groups and communities with associated risk.

12.3 Regularly monitor, re-assess, and manage risk to individuals, families, carers, groups and communities.

Unit 13 – Assess, minimise and manage risk to self and colleagues
13.1 Assess potential risk to self and colleagues.
13.2 Work within the risk assessment and management procedures of your own and other relevant organisations and professions.
13.3 Plan, monitor and review outcomes and actions to minimise stress and risk.

Key Role 5: Manage and be accountable, with supervision and support, for your own social work practice within your organisation

Unit 14 – Manage and be accountable for your own work
14.1 Manage and prioritise your workload within organisational policies and priorities.
14.2 Carry out duties using accountable professional judgment and knowledge based social work practice.
14.3 Monitor and evaluate the effectiveness of your programme of work in meeting the organisational requirements and the needs of individuals, families, carers, groups and communities.
14.4 Use professional and managerial supervision and support to improve your practice.

Unit 15 – Contribute to the management of resources and services
15.1 Contribute to the procedures involved in purchasing and commissioning services.
15.2 Contribute to monitoring the effectiveness of services in meeting need.
15.3 Contribute to monitoring the quality of the services provided.
15.4 Contribute to managing information.

Unit 16 – Manage, present and share records and reports
16.1 Maintain accurate, complete, accessible, and up-to-date records and reports.
16.2 Provide evidence for judgments and decisions.
16.3 Implement legal and policy frameworks for access to records and reports.
16.4 Share records with individuals, families, carers, groups and communities.

Unit 17 – Work within multi-disciplinary and multi-organisational teams, networks and systems
17.1 Develop and maintain effective working relationships.
17.2 Contribute to identifying and agreeing the goals, objectives and lifespan of the team, network or system.
17.3 Contribute to evaluating the effectiveness of the team, network or system.
17.4 Deal constructively with disagreements and conflict within relationships.

Key Role 6: Demonstrate professional competence in social work practice
Unit 18 – Research, analyse, evaluate, and use current knowledge of best social work practice
18.1 Review and update your own knowledge of legal, policy and procedural frameworks.
18.2 Use professional and organisational supervision and support to research, critically analyse, and review knowledge based practice.
18.3 Implement knowledge based social work models and methods to develop and improve your own practice.

Unit 19 – Work within agreed standards of social work practice and ensure own professional development
19.1 Exercise and justify professional judgements.
19.2 Use professional assertiveness to justify decisions and uphold professional social work practice, values and ethics.
19.3 Work within the principles and values underpinning social work practice.
19.4 Critically reflect upon your own practice and performance using supervision and support systems.
19.5 Use supervision and support to take action to meet continuing professional development needs.

Unit 20 – Manage complex ethical issues, dilemmas and conflicts
20.1 Identify and assess issues, dilemmas and conflicts that might affect your practice.
20.2 Devise strategies to deal with ethical issues, dilemmas and conflicts.
20.3 Reflect on outcomes.

Unit 21 – Contribute to the promotion of best social work practice

21.1 Contribute to policy review and development.

21.2 Use supervision and organisational and professional systems to inform a course of action where practice falls below required standards.

21.3 Work with colleagues to contribute to team development.

Appendix 2
Subject benchmark for social work

Nature and extent of social work
3.5 Honours degree programmes in social work may be studied full-time, part-time, open and distance learning, work-based, and post-experience modes. Irrespective of learning mode, all honours degree programmes covered by this statement must include structured opportunities for supervised or directed practice in relevant and appropriate practice-learning settings.

Defining principles
4.5 The applied nature of social work as an academic subject means that practice is an essential and core element of learning.

Subject-specific skills and other skills
5.2 As an applied subject at honours degree level, social work necessarily involves the development of skills that may be of value in many situations (for example, analytical thinking, building relationships, working as a member of an organisation, intervention, evaluation and reflection). Some of these skills are specific to social work but many are also widely transferable. What helps to define the specific nature of these skills in a social work context are:
- the context in which they are applied and assessed (e.g., communication skills in practice with people with sensory impairments or assessment skills in an interprofessional setting);
- the relative weighting given to such skills within social work practice (e.g., the central importance of problem-solving skills within complex human situations);
- the specific purpose of skill development (e.g., the acquisition of research skills in order to build a repertoire of research-based practice);
- a requirement to integrate a range of skills (i.e., not simply to demonstrate these in an isolated and incremental manner).

5.3 All social work honours graduates should show the ability to reflect on and learn from the exercise of their skills. They should understand the significance of the concepts of continuing professional development and lifelong learning, and accept responsibility for their own continuing development.

5.4 Social work honours graduates should acquire and integrate skills in the following five core areas

Problem-solving skills
5.5 These are sub-divided into four areas.
5.5.1 Managing problem-solving activities: honours graduates in social work should
be able to plan problem-solving activities, i.e. to:

- think logically, systematically, critically and reflectively;

- apply ethical principles and practices critically in planning problem-solving activities;

- plan a sequence of actions to achieve specified objectives, making use of research, theory and other forms of evidence;

- manage processes of change, drawing on research, theory and other forms of evidence.

5.5.2 Gathering information: honours graduates in social work should be able to:

- gather information from a wide range of sources and by a variety of methods, for a range of purposes. These methods should include electronic searches, reviews of relevant literature, policy and procedures, face-to-face interviews, written and telephone contact with individuals and groups;

- take into account differences of viewpoint in gathering information and critically assess the reliability and relevance of the information gathered;

- assimilate and disseminate relevant information in reports and case records.

5.5.3 Analysis and synthesis: honours graduates in social work should be able to analyse and synthesise knowledge gathered for problem-solving purposes, i.e., to:

- assess human situations, taking into account a variety of factors (including the views of participants, theoretical concepts, research evidence, legislation and organisational policies and procedures);

- analyse information gathered, weighing competing evidence and modifying their viewpoint in light of new information, then relate this information to a particular task, situation or problem;

- consider specific factors relevant to social work practice (such as risk, rights, cultural differences and linguistic sensitivities, responsibilities to protect vulnerable individuals and legal obligations);

- assess the merits of contrasting theories, explanations, research, policies and procedures;

- synthesise knowledge and sustain reasoned argument;

- employ a critical understanding of human agency at the macro (societal), mezzo (organisational and community) and micro (inter and intrapersonal) levels;

- critically analyse and take account of the impact of inequality and discrimination in work with people in particular contexts and problem situations.

5.5.4 Intervention and evaluation: honours graduates in social work should be able to
use their knowledge of a range of interventions and evaluation processes selectively to:

- build and sustain purposeful relationships with people and organisations in community-based, and interprofessional contexts;

- make decisions, set goals and construct specific plans to achieve these, taking into account relevant factors including ethical guidelines;

- negotiate goals and plans with others, analysing and addressing in a creative manner human, organisational and structural impediments to change;

- implement plans through a variety of systematic processes that include working in partnership;

- undertake practice in a manner that promotes the well-being and protects the safety of all parties;

- engage effectively in conflict resolution;

- support service users to take decisions and access services, with the social worker as navigator, advocate and supporter;

- manage the complex dynamics of dependency and, in some settings, provide direct care and personal support in everyday living situations;

- meet deadlines and comply with external definitions of a task;

- plan, implement and critically review processes and outcomes;

- bring work to an effective conclusion, taking into account the implications for all involved;

- monitor situations, review processes and evaluate outcomes;

- use and evaluate methods of intervention critically and reflectively.

Communication skills

5.6 Honours graduates in social work should be able to communicate clearly, accurately and precisely (in an appropriate medium) with individuals and groups in a range of formal and informal situations, i.e., to:

- make effective contact with individuals and organisations for a range of objectives, by verbal, paper-based and electronic means;

- clarify and negotiate the purpose of such contacts and the boundaries of their involvement;

- listen actively to others, engage appropriately with the life experiences of service users, understand accurately their viewpoint and overcome personal prejudices to respond appropriately to a range of complex personal and interpersonal situations;

- use both verbal and non-verbal cues to guide interpretation;

- identify and use opportunities for purposeful and supportive communication with service users within their everyday living situations;

- follow and develop an argument and evaluate the viewpoints of, and evidence presented by, others;

- write accurately and clearly in styles adapted to the audience, purpose and context of the communication;

- use advocacy skills to promote others' rights, interests and needs;

- present conclusions verbally and on paper, in a structured form, appropriate to the audience for which these have been prepared;

- make effective preparation for, and lead meetings in a productive way;

- communicate effectively across potential barriers resulting from differences (e.g., in culture, language and age).

Skills in personal and professional development

5.8 Honours graduates in social work should be able to:

- advance their own learning and understanding with a degree of independence;

- reflect on and modify their behaviour in the light of experience;

- identify and keep under review their own personal and professional boundaries;

- manage uncertainty, change and stress in work situations;

- handle inter- and intrapersonal conflict constructively;

- understand and manage changing situations and respond in a flexible manner;

- challenge unacceptable practices in a responsible manner;

- take responsibility for their own further and continuing acquisition and use of knowledge and skills;

- use research critically and effectively to sustain and develop their practice.

Teaching, learning and assessment

6.2 The learning processes in social work at honours degree level can be expressed in terms of four inter-related themes.

- Awareness raising, skills and knowledge acquisition – a process in which the student becomes more aware of aspects of knowledge and expertise, learns how to systematically engage with and acquire new areas of knowledge, recognises their potential and becomes motivated to engage in new ways of thinking and acting.

- Conceptual understanding – a process in which a student acquires, examines critically and deepens understanding (measured and tested against existing knowledge and adjustments made in attitudes and goals).

- Practice skills and experience – processes in which a student learns practice skills in the contexts identified in paragraph 4.4 and applies theoretical models and research evidence together with new understanding to relevant activities, and receives feedback from various sources on performance, enhancing openness to critical self-evaluation.

- Reflection on performance – a process in which a student reflects critically and evaluatively on past experience, recent performance and feedback, and applies this information to the process of integrating awareness (including awareness of the impact of self on others) and new understanding, leading to improved performance.

Subject-specific and other skills

7.1 Given the essentially applied nature of social work and the co-terminosity of the degree and the professional award, students must demonstrate that they have met the standards specified in relation to both academic and practice capabilities. These standards relate to subject-specific knowledge, understanding and skills (including key skills inherent in the concept of 'graduateness'). Qualifying students will be expected to meet each of these standards in accordance with the specific standards set by the relevant country (see section 2).

7.4 On graduating with an honours degree in social work, students should be able to demonstrate a developed capacity to:

- apply creatively a repertoire of core skills as detailed in section 5;

- communicate effectively with service users and carers, and with other professionals;

- integrate clear understanding of ethical issues and codes of values, and practice with their interventions in specific situations;

- consistently exercise an appropriate level of autonomy and initiative in individual decision-making within the context of supervisory, collaborative, ethical and organisational requirements;

- demonstrate habits of critical reflection on their performance and take responsibility for modifying action in light of this.

Appendix 3
GSCC's codes of practice for social care workers

Please note for the sake of brevity only the code for social care workers is reproduced here. For sight of the codes for employees of social care workers please go to the General Social Care Council's website.

The purpose of this code is to set out the conduct that is expected of social care workers and to inform service users and the public about the standards of conduct they can expect from social care workers. It forms part of the wider package of legislation, practice standards and employers' policies and procedures that social care workers must meet. Social care workers are responsible for making sure that their conduct does not fall below the standards set out in this code and that no action or omission on their part harms the wellbeing of service users.

Status

The General Social Care Council expects social care workers to meet this code and may take action if registered workers fail to do so.

Employers of social care workers are required to take account of this code in making any decisions about the conduct of their staff.

Social care workers must:

- Protect the rights and promote the interests of service users and carers.

- Strive to establish and maintain the trust and confidence of service users and carers.

- Promote the independence of service users while protecting them as far as possible from danger or harm.

- Respect the rights of service users whilst seeking to ensure that their behaviour does not harm themselves or other people.

- Uphold public trust and confidence in social care services.

- Be accountable for the quality of their work and take responsibility for maintaining and improving their knowledge and skills.

1 As a social care worker, you must protect the rights and promote the interests of service users and carers. This includes:

1.1 Treating each person as an individual.

1.2 Respecting and, where appropriate, promoting the individual views and wishes of both service users and carers.

1.3 Supporting service users' rights to control their lives and make informed choices about the services they receive.

1.4 Respecting and maintaining the dignity and privacy of service users.

1.5 Promoting equal opportunities for service users and carers.

1.6 Respecting diversity and different cultures and values.

2 As a social care worker, you must strive to establish and maintain the trust and confidence of service users and carers. This includes:

2.1 Being honest and trustworthy.

2.2 Communicating in an appropriate, open, accurate and straightforward way.

2.3 Respecting confidential information and clearly explaining agency policies about confidentiality to service users and carers.

2.4 Being reliable and dependable.

2.5 Honouring work commitments, agreements and arrangements and, when it is not possible to do so, explaining why to service users and carers.

2.6 Declaring issues that might create conflicts of interest and making sure that they do not influence your judgement or practice.

2.7 Adhering to policies and procedures about accepting gifts and money from service users and carers.

3 As a social care worker, you must promote the independence of service users while protecting them as far as possible from danger or harm. This includes:

3.1 Promoting the independence of service users and assisting them to understand and exercise their rights.

3.2 Using established processes and procedures to challenge and report dangerous, abusive, discriminatory or exploitative behaviour and practice.

3.3 Following practice and procedures designed to keep you and other people safe from violent and abusive behaviour at work.

3.4 Bringing to the attention of your employer or the appropriate authority resource or operational difficulties that might get in the way of the delivery of safe care.

3.5 Informing your employer or an appropriate authority where the practice of colleagues may be unsafe or adversely affecting standards of care.

3.6 Complying with employers' health and safety policies, including those relating to substance abuse.

3.7 Helping service users and carers to make complaints, taking complaints seriously and responding to them or passing them to the appropriate person.

3.8 Recognising and using responsibly the power that comes from your work with service users and carers.

4 As a social care worker, you must respect the rights of service users while seeking to ensure that their behaviour does not harm themselves or other people. This includes:

4.1 Recognising that service users have the right to take risks and helping them to identify and manage potential and actual risks to themselves and others.

4.2 Following risk assessment policies and procedures to assess whether the behaviour of service users presents a risk of harm to themselves or others.

4.3 Taking necessary steps to minimise the risks of service users from doing actual or potential harm to themselves or other people.

4.4 Ensuring that relevant colleagues and agencies are informed about the outcomes and implications of risk assessments.

5 As a social care worker, you must uphold public trust and confidence in social care services. In particular you must not:

5.1 Abuse, neglect or harm service users, carers or colleagues.

5.2 Exploit service users, carers or colleagues in any way.

5.3 Abuse the trust of service users and carers or the access you have to personal information about them or to their property, home or workplace.

5.4 Form inappropriate personal relationships with service users.

5.5 Discriminate unlawfully or unjustifiably against service users, carers or colleagues.

5.6 Condone any unlawful or unjustifiable discrimination by service users, carers or colleagues.

5.7 Put yourself or other people at unnecessary risk.

5.8 Behave in a way, in work or outside work, which would call into question your suitability to work in social care services.

6 As a social care worker, you must be accountable for the quality of your work and take responsibility for maintaining and improving your knowledge and skills. This includes:

6.1 Meeting relevant standards of practice and working in a lawful, safe and effective way.

6.2 Maintaining clear and accurate records as required by procedures established for your work.

6.3 Informing your employer or the appropriate authority about any personal difficulties that might affect your ability to do your job competently and safely.

6.4 Seeking assistance from your employer or the appropriate authority if you do not feel able or adequately prepared to carry out any aspect of your work, or you are not sure about how to proceed in a work matter.

6.5 Working openly and cooperatively with colleagues and treating them with respect.

6.6 Recognising that you remain responsible for the work that you have delegated to other workers.

6.7 Recognising and respecting the roles and expertise of workers from other agencies and working in partnership with them.

6.8 Undertaking relevant training to maintain and improve your knowledge and skills and contributing to the learning and development of others.

References

Bourd, D, Keogh, R and Walker, D (1985) *Reflection: Turning experience into learning.* London: Kogan Page.

Brockbank, A and McGill, I (1998) *Facilitating reflective learning in higher education.* Buckingham: SRHE/Open University Press.

Cotterell, S (2004) *The study skills handbook,* 2nd edition. Basingstoke: Palgrave.

Darn, S (2005) Aspects of nonverbal communication. *Internet TESL journal, XI (2)* [online]. **http://iteslj.org/Articles/ Darn-Nonverbal/**

Department of Health, Department for Education and Employment, and the Home Office (2000) *Framework for the assessment of children in need and their families.* London: The Stationery Office. Available at **www.dh.gov.uk/**.

Eraut, M (1994) *Developing professional knowledge and competence.* Abingdon: Falmer Press.

Fisher, T and Somerton, J (2000) Reflection on action: The process of helping social work students to develop their use of theory in practice. *Social Work Education,* 19 (4), 387–401.

General Social Care Council (2002) *Codes of practice for social workers and employers.* London: GSCC.

Lishman, J (2009) *Communication in social work.* Basingstoke: Palgrave Macmillan.

Lomax, R, Jones, K, Leigh, S and Gay, C (2010) *Surviving your social work placement.* Basingstoke: Palgrave Macmillan.

Maclean, S and Harrison, R (2009) *Making the most of your practice learning opportunities.* Rugeley: Kirwin Maclean Associates.

Moon, J (2004) *A handbook for reflective and experiential learning.* Abingdon: Routledge.

Northedge, A (2005) *The good study guide.* 2nd edition. Buckingham: Open University Press.

Parker, J (2010) *Effective practice learning in social work.* 2nd edition. Exeter: Learning Matters.

Peck, J and Coyle, M (eds.) (2005) *Write it right: A handbook for students.* Basingstoke: Palgrave.

Quality Assurance Agency for Higher Education (2008) *Benchmark statements for social work.* **www.qaa.ac.uk** (accessed 28 March 2011).

Social Work Reform Board (2010) *Building a safe and confident future: One year on* – Detailed proposal from the Social Work Reform Board. London: Department for Education. Available at **www.education.gov.uk/publications/**.

SWAP (Social Policy and Social Work) (2007) SWAP guide 3: *The social work degree: Preparing to succeed.* **www.swap.ac.uk**

Thorpe, M (2000) Encouraging students to reflect as part of the assignment process. *Active learning in higher education,* 1 (1), 79–92.

Topss UK Partnership (2002) *National Occupational Standards for Social Work.* **www.skillsforcare.org.uk**

Walker, H (2011) *Studying for your social work degree.* Exeter: 2nd edition. Learning Matters.

Index